Hands-On Engineering

Real-World Projects for the Classroom

D1509417

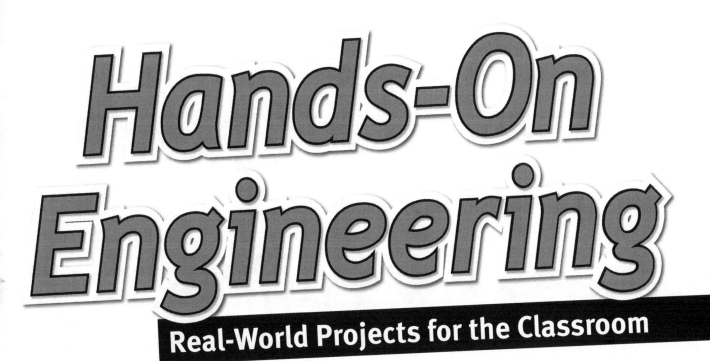

Hands-On Engineering

Real-World Projects for the Classroom

Beth L. Andrews

PRUFROCK PRESS INC.
WACO, TEXAS

Dedication

I dedicate this book to my best friend and husband, Jeff. Whether becalmed or amid a tempest, he is the keel that allows me to stay the course.

Copyright ©2012 Prufrock Press Inc.

Edited by Sarah Morrison

Production design by Raquel Trevino
Illustrations by Joshua Krezinski

ISBN-13: 978-1-59363-922-8

Prufrock Press Inc.
P.O. Box 8813
Waco, TX 76714-8813
Phone: (800) 998-2208
Fax: (800) 240-0333
http://www.prufrock.com

Table of Contents

Introduction

Design and Engineering

We are all designers and engineers. We are constantly faced with situations that require us to analyze problems and to work for solutions. Since the beginning of recorded history, every aspect of humankind's survival has been influenced by the principles of design. Humans have been designing methods of survival and modifying those methods to be more effective since early humans first developed the fundamental tools with which they lived. Look around you right now. Which designs and ideas are integral parts of your world, and how might your life be different without those designs and ideas?

Engineers are innovators who look at how the world works. They investigate how buildings stand up, how bacteria is removed from drinking water, how systems are developed to help people, how machines work, and how people build and use technology. There are constantly new problems to solve and processes to streamline in engineering.

Engineering is a form of design, and design is a component of engineering. They overlap and complement one another depending on the situation. *Design* is defined as both the conception of an idea in the mind and the invention and formulation of a plan. *Engineering*, on the other hand, is defined as the application of given principles (e.g., scientific, mathematical) in order to achieve practical ends, such as designing, making, and operating structures, machines, methods, and systems. Design and engineering are both necessary in solving problems that focus on transportation, food, shelter, space, environment, weather, entertainment, and other components of human life as we know it.

Why is it important to understand the principles of engineering and design? The art of design allows us to exist in today's world. The basic fundamentals of our ways of life are constantly changing; therefore, the design process is a never-ending journey of discovery. Designers develop a different lens through which to see the world. Observations and insights allow designers and engineers to see what works well, what needs to be modified, and what needs to be invented or created.

How are we, as educators, providing the tools and strategies that our students need in order to learn about and understand these essential design concepts and skills so that one day they may improve people's lives? In today's academic climate of standardized tests and performance-based achievement, students often learn how to arrive at a single correct answer. Machines are able to produce calculations and facts; people, however, must understand how to approach a problem with multiple perspectives and innovative solutions, as well as how to integrate a given solution into the current system or climate. The fact that people will always need to invent new solutions and design new technology and methodology renders the teaching of design and engineering not only practical and useful, but also highly necessary.

Exposing students to design methodologies through hands-on experiences enables the designers of our future world to connect intuitively with the subject matter and to create through careful consideration and analysis. When we allow our students to think, they are nurturing the designers within. In this way, we are preparing today's students to become productive citizens—responsible community members who are able to work collaboratively to solve real, consequential problems.

The Realm of Design and Engineering

Design and engineering involve applying skills and knowledge to a problem that requires a change in environment in order to make it more accessible, pleasing, efficient, or effective. To put it in simpler terms, design and engineering involve identifying and solving a problem.

In today's 21st-century world, it is more important than ever to ensure that our students are equipped to use the analytical thinking characteristic of the design and engineering process. Increasingly, even careers not traditionally thought to fall into the realm of design and engineering nevertheless demand design- and engineering-related skills such as analysis, teamwork, creativity, and innovation. Even a more traditional list of the areas that fall under the umbrella of design and engineering is quite extensive and includes the following disciplines:

Business	Product Development	Packaging	Gaming Industry
Software	Web Design	Communication	Electrical Engineering
Sound	Functional Design	Structural Design	Architecture

Automotive Industry	Cellular Manufacturing	Environmental Issues	Interior Design
Commercial Industry	Urban Development	Mechanical Industry	Artistic Design

With design and engineering playing a pivotal role in so many fields and professions, educators owe it to their students to teach design and engineering principles, as well as to foster a curiosity about the tenets of design and engineering. The larger scale solutions associated with design and engineering problems may not be traditionally associated with the simpler solutions required on standardized tests, but the skills and lessons of design and engineering will enable students to apply analytical and creative thinking not just to standardized tests, but to challenges they face throughout their lives.

The Design and Engineering Process

The process of design and engineering depends on an individual's general philosophy. Some people may prefer to include a guide detailing their specific methods, for instance, whereas other people may prefer to alter their course throughout the process. Although there is no discrete, correct way to design, there are certain methods that help to organize the process. If you have students who like structuring the way they work, they may benefit from a discussion of the various approaches to the design and engineering process.

The Rational Model, developed by pioneers in the field of science and design, suggests three truths pertaining to the concept of design:
1. The design's purpose is to improve upon something.
2. The design's process is driven by a plan.
3. The design's process is understood in terms of a separate sequence of stages.

There are four stages in the Rational Model:
1. In **preproduction**, the design is set in motion.
2. During **production**, a design solution is developed and tested.
3. In **postproduction**, the design is implemented and evaluated.
4. In the **redesign** phase, the design is corrected and redone.

During the preproduction stage, the path of the design is set in motion. The first step is the design *brief*, or statement of goals. Once the goals have been stated, an *analysis* of current design goals needs to be completed, as well as research of similar design solutions in the field. After completing the analysis, the designer is ready to provide specification of a design *solution* for a product or service. From there, the designer begins problem solving. When the problems have been considered and addressed, the ideas are presented.

Postproduction is an important stage for designers. It is during this stage that the designer provides feedback for future designs. The implementation and introduction of the designed solution into the environment take place during the postproduction. A thorough evaluation is completed, and a summary of the process and results is offered, including constructive criticism and suggestions for future improvements. Although redesign is designated as the final stage, this stage may actually occur at any time during the design process. During the redesign, specific components of the design process are repeated and corrections are made.

Other design approaches include the following:

1. The KISS principle (Keep It Simple and Sequential), which emphasizes the importance of eliminating the burden of following too many rules throughout a process.
2. TIMTOWTDI (There Is More Than One Way To Do It), a philosophy that allows for a variety of methods of accomplishing a given end or solving a given problem.
3. The Engineering Design Process: Ask, Imagine, Plan, Create, and Improve.
   a. Ask
      i. What is the problem?
      ii. What has been done before?
      iii. What worked, and what did not work?
      iv. What are the boundaries or constraints?
   b. Imagine
      i. What are some possible solutions?
      ii. What are some ideas?
      iii. Which single idea seems like the best one for this situation?
   c. Plan
      i. Draw a diagram.
      ii. Make lists of materials needed.
      iii. Anticipate obstacles and work out bugs.
   d. Create
      i. Follow your plan and create it.
      ii. Test your plan.
      iii. Modify your plan as necessary.
   e. Improve
      i. Talk about what works, what doesn't work, and what could work better.

    ii.   Analyze similar designs.

    iii.   Modify your design to make it better.

    iv.   Test it out again.

What do students learn when studying design and engineering? In addition to teaching important design and engineering principles, design-based lessons teach important scientific principles and mathematical concepts. Through project-based learning experiences, students are challenged to think critically about solving real-life problems using innovative techniques. They are able to apply creative and critical thinking to each activity. What problems exist today that could be solved with improved designs? What inventions are just around the corner that will improve our quality of life? What potential dangers lurk on the floors of our oceans? What possible disasters and inventions could be brewing in the core of the Earth? What issues can be observed on the surface of our planet? Everywhere we look, there is a need for designers and engineers.

Standards and the STEM Initiative

The activities in *Hands-On Engineering* were designed to align with various standards for science, technology, engineering, and mathematics (STEM). The current emphasis in schools on STEM disciplines is meant to prepare students for technology-rich occupations in a more globally sophisticated world. According to the National Governors Association (2007), STEM supports educational models "that focus on rigor and relevance to ensure that every student is STEM literate upon graduation from high school, and a greater number of students move onto postsecondary education and training in STEM disciplines" (p. 3). As students work through the challenges in this book, they will be meeting the math, science, and technology standards set forth by the International Society for Technology in Education (2008), the International Technology Education Association (2007), the National Council of Teachers of Mathematics (2000), and the National Research Council (1996). The essential goals of this book overlap with the goals set forth by the STEM initiative:

- ◆ Make students better problem solvers, enabling them to define questions, solve problems, design investigations, gather data, organize data, draw conclusions, and apply their findings to novel situations.
- ◆ Encourage students to be innovators who creatively use science, math, and technology and apply them to the engineering and design processes.

- ◆ Foster an inventive spirit in students such that they recognize the world's problems and needs and think of how to design, test, redesign, and implement practical solutions.
- ◆ Increase students' self-reliance so that they are able to use initiative and self-motivation to make agendas, gain confidence in their abilities, and work within set timeframes.
- ◆ Lead students to think logically and apply the rational thought processes of science, mathematics, and engineering.
- ◆ Guide students towards technological literacy so that they understand the nature of relevant technology and are able to develop and apply the skills needed to use that technology.

Hands-On Engineering Challenges

Features of the Challenges

Each challenge gives students the opportunity to design an object or structure while keeping in mind a given objective. For each challenge, there are step-by-step instructions for teachers to follow in their own classrooms, including links to websites that will help introduce the concepts that students will need to understand before completing the given task. If you are unable to use the links provided in the lessons (i.e., if you do not have a computer with Internet access or you are unable to access the websites listed), you may adapt the challenges so that you can preview or review the relevant concepts as necessary with your students without the use of Internet resources. Each challenge also includes a ready-to-use worksheet that students will complete first individually and then in teams. This worksheet will allow you to assign grades based not only on team accomplishments, but also on individual work, ideas, and reflection. Following each challenge is a section detailing how you might extend the learning in your classroom. For some challenges, this section takes the form of a worksheet with various options on it that you may distribute to students and assign to be completed outside of class. For other challenges, the extended learning section focuses on an in-depth project that you could offer to your students, tailoring it to fit your classroom.

Additionally, your purchase of this book entitles you to download a companion document (PDF format) containing the following for each lesson:

- ◆ a list of clickable links to the websites used in the lesson (to make them more easily accessible),

◆ a list of additional resources you might use to extend the lesson or to focus on certain topics, and

◆ a list of some of the sources used to create the lesson (should you wish to use these sources as additional reading).

To download the online companion document to this book, please visit: http://www.prufrock.com/assets/ClientPages/hands_on_eng.aspx

Use in the Classroom

Read through all of the *Hands-On Engineering* challenge activities, and then select which ones match your students' needs and best align with your curriculum and standards. The challenges have been ordered so that the earlier ones are easier, whereas the later ones require more background knowledge and additional math and science skills. Whether or not you adhere to the suggested order of the challenges depends on how much your students already know, as well as your own familiarity with the material. Some of the challenges are similar in terms of the products that students are making (e.g., a paper airplane and a stealth aircraft, a boat and a raft), but the difference lies in the design. For instance, a boat's hull is angled, whereas a raft uses a flat base. The paper airplane has a longer body than does the stealth aircraft, which is square. These variations in design are important and give students a clearer understanding about what implications such variations have with regard to aerodynamics, buoyancy, and so forth.

Students will work individually during the instructional portion, and they will work collaboratively with peers throughout the design and engineering elements (although you could make modifications in order to allow for individual or whole-class work). You may prefer to assign teams, depending on your students' ability levels and characteristics, or you may allow students to choose their own teams. The number of students on each team will vary depending on the requirements of the challenge (most challenges work best when students are in teams of three). Of course, you can also vary how you group students depending on the challenge, and there is much flexibility in terms of how you adapt these lessons and activities for your classroom.

Materials

The purpose of this book is to provide opportunities for students to utilize engineering concepts, ideas of physical and environmental science, and high-level mathematical skills through creative activities. To this end, they will not use expensive equipment, but rather everyday materials that can be found around the classroom or can be donated at the beginning of the school year. The letter provided on page 11 could be distributed at back-to-school night to help you accumulate materials for your classroom. A corresponding checklist has been provided that you can hang in your classroom near where you store the collected materials. The materials list accompanying each lesson can be modified to include any other materials you have on hand and think would be useful for a particular challenge. When you are preparing the materials for a challenge, it works well to place the materials in two different areas in the classroom so that the students don't form a mob as they try to obtain what they need for the challenge (they often get quite worked up when there is a time limit involved!). Also, it may be helpful to tell students that each team may only send one team member to retrieve the materials; this will also prevent mobs from forming and will allow the other teammates to begin work on their designs.

Preparation

The following list includes items to keep in mind as you prepare to begin implementing the *Hands-On Engineering* challenges in your classroom.

1. Before conducting each activity, make sure that you have gathered the required materials. It is useful if you provide a shelf or a large box for keeping track of materials. Place the provided Materials Inventory List (p. 10) or a list that you have created near this storage spot to keep tabs on what you already have and what you will need to gather prior to conducting a given activity. The Materials Collection Request letter provided on page 11 can be used as a template to collect materials for the challenge activities, although you may wish to create your own letter or use a different means of collecting materials.

2. Two lessons, Kite for a Windy Day (p. 120) and It's Getting Hot in Here (p. 158), require specific weather conditions in order to be completed. The former, a kite challenge, requires a windy day (although a fan could be used as an alternative), and the latter, a solar oven challenge, requires a sunny, hot day.

3. Each challenge activity can be completed in either one or two blocks of time, depending on your schedule. For some challenges, you may wish to allocate additional time and make modifications to allow for more in-depth learning.

4. All challenge activities may be completed individually, in partners, or as a class, if you make modifications. When used as written, most of the challenges are designed to have students work in teams of three.

5. Be sure to review every challenge in advance. You will need to prepare a challenge site, adapt for your students' skill level and knowledge, and make any other necessary adjustments.

6. Most of the challenges require students to transport their designs to a challenge site. Remind students of this so that they do not construct immovable designs!

7. Because some of the challenges are structured differently (e.g., some challenges require students to collect data as the challenges are occurring, whereas others do not), also review the student worksheet for each challenge in advance so that you can monitor students and give them helpful reminders as they complete their activity sheets.

Materials Inventory List

Check off items as they arrive.

- ❑ 8.5" x 11" Paper
- ❑ Beads
- ❑ Cardboard Tubing
- ❑ Clay
- ❑ Coffee Containers
- ❑ Corks
- ❑ Egg Cartons
- ❑ Film Canisters
- ❑ Gardening Sticks
- ❑ Golf Balls
- ❑ Index Cards
- ❑ Labels
- ❑ Marbles
- ❑ Metersticks/Yardsticks
- ❑ Newspaper
- ❑ Paper Clips
- ❑ Paper Plates
- ❑ Plastic Garbage Bags
- ❑ Play Dough
- ❑ Rubber Bands
- ❑ Self-Adhesive Dots
- ❑ Spools
- ❑ String
- ❑ Tape
- ❑ Twine

- ❑ 9" x 12" Construction Paper
- ❑ Cardboard
- ❑ CDs
- ❑ Clothespins
- ❑ Containers (Various Shapes)
- ❑ Dowels
- ❑ Fabric Scraps
- ❑ Foil
- ❑ Glue
- ❑ Graph Paper
- ❑ Jar Lids
- ❑ Large Buttons
- ❑ Metal Brads
- ❑ Miscellaneous Items
- ❑ Paper Bowls
- ❑ Paper Cups
- ❑ Pennies
- ❑ Plastic Spoons
- ❑ Popsicle Sticks
- ❑ Rulers
- ❑ Shoe Boxes
- ❑ Straws
- ❑ Styrofoam Plates
- ❑ Toothpicks
- ❑ Yarn

Materials Collection Request

Dear Parent,

As part of our math and science curriculum, our class will be participating in *Hands-On Engineering*, a series of design and engineering challenges that utilize engineering concepts, the principles of physical and environmental science, high-level mathematical skills, and creativity. The purpose of these challenges is to provide important practice in applying scientific ideas and mathematical skills while finding creative solutions to a variety of real-life problems. By the end of this school year, your child will be able to think more analytically, scientifically, mathematically, and creatively.

In order to conduct these challenges, we will need a variety of everyday materials. Please look around your home for items on this list that you can donate to our class to use for our challenges. If you can think of other items that may be helpful, please send those in as well, provided they are in keeping with the school's safety regulations.

Materials Needed

8.5" x 11" Paper	9" x 12" Construction Paper	Beads	Cardboard	Cardboard Tubing
CDs	Clay	Clothespins	Coffee Containers	Containers (Various Shapes)
Corks	Dowels	Egg Cartons	Fabric Scraps	Film Canisters
Foil	Gardening Sticks	Glue	Golf Balls	Graph Paper
Index Cards	Jar Lids	Labels	Large Buttons	Marbles
Metal Brads	Metersticks/Yardsticks	Miscellaneous Items	Newspaper	Paper Bowls
Paper Clips	Paper Cups	Paper Plates	Pennies	Plastic Garbage Bags
Plastic Spoons	Play Dough	Popsicle Sticks	Rubber Bands	Rulers
Self-Adhesive Dots	Shoe Boxes	Spools	Straws	String
Styrofoam Plates	Tape	Toothpicks	Twine	Yarn

Thank you for your time. Your donations are greatly appreciated, and they will be very helpful in our efforts to solve real-world design and engineering challenges.

Sincerely,

Please cut on this line and send in the below portion with your donated materials.

- -

I have read the letter regarding *Hands-On Engineering*. The materials I have sent in include:

1. _____   2. _____

3. _____   4. _____

5. _____   6. _____

Student's Signature: _____

Parent's Signature: _____ Date: _____

The Good Old-Fashioned Paper Airplane

Make an airplane that achieves the longest straight flight when released.

Subjects and Skills

- Measurement
- Calculating averages
- Aerodynamics

Materials

- 8.5" x 11" paper (one sheet per student for individual activity and one sheet per team in group activity)
- Metersticks/yardsticks
- An area in which students can throw paper airplanes (e.g., gymnasium, field)

Vocabulary

- Aerodynamics
- Aviation

Purpose

This activity will improve students' ability to:
- understand the fundamentals of aerodynamics,
- apply principles of aerodynamics to objects moving through air,
- apply distance-measurement skills,
- convert standard measurements, and
- calculate averages.

Objectives

Students will demonstrate:
- an understanding of aerodynamics by creating a paper airplane,
- the ability to measure to the nearest eighth of an inch, and
- the ability to calculate averages.

Activity Preparation

1. Run off activity sheet.
2. Gather materials and place them in two different areas in the room.
3. Bookmark websites to be used in class.
   a. http://teachertech.rice.edu/Participants/louviere/Newton
   b. http://www.physicsclassroom.com/mmedia/newtlaws/cci.cfm
   c. http://auto.howstuffworks.com/fuel-efficiency/fuel-economy/aerodynamics1.htm

Activity Procedure

1. Begin the discussion by asking the students if they have ever wondered how a heavy object, like an airplane, can fly in the air. Introduce Sir Isaac Newton and his law of gravity. Visit Link a. and Link b. in order to introduce Newton's achievements and contributions.
2. Discuss how aerodynamics works by displacing air around an object. Visit sites that provide examples and a more thorough explanation, including Link c.
3. Pass out the activity sheet for students to continue the lesson.
4. After students have completed their individual airplanes, allow them to complete a test flight and then record their results.
5. Divide students into groups of two or three to complete the challenge, and give each group a team number.
6. Allow the groups to settle and discuss their plans before beginning the challenge. Hold the challenge in whatever manner is easiest and most appropriate for your classroom.
7. After the competition, have students complete the activity sheet.
8. If you wish, assign one of the projects suggested in Extend the Learning With Aerodynamics: Project Ideas.

The Good Old-Fashioned Paper Airplane

The Good Old-Fashioned Paper Airplane

GOAL

➢ Make an airplane that achieves the longest straight flight when released.

MATERIALS

➢ 8.5" x 11" paper (one sheet per student for individual activity and one sheet per team in group activity)

TIME TO CREATE

➢ 12 minutes

INDIVIDUAL ACTIVITY

Read the following information, answer the questions, and follow the instructions.

What is aerodynamics?

Use a dictionary to determine the relationship of the two Greek words that make up the word aerodynamics:

aerios, meaning _____,

and *dynamis*, meaning _____.

Aerodynamics is _____

_____.

Although humans have been interested in aerodynamics and aviation for thousands of years, flying in a "heavier-than-air" craft has only been possible in the last century. Every airplane flight, bicycle ride, model rocket launch, kite expedition, automobile drive, and baseball pitch is designed around the basic concepts of aerodynamics.

Thinking about aerodynamics brings us to the task at hand. You will make your own paper airplane, following the instructions. If you know how to make a more efficient paper airplane, then include directions on the back of this sheet. You may follow your own design instructions after first building a paper airplane according to the guidelines. You can feel free to experiment and share your ideas after the competition. However, to ensure fairness, all airplanes entered in this challenge must adhere to these directions.

1. Fold an 8.5" x 11" sheet of paper in half lengthwise (like a hot dog).
2. Fold the short edge of one side down to the crease to produce a 45-degree angle. Repeat this step on the other side.
3. Fold the new fold you have created to the original fold you did in Step 1. Repeat on the other side.
4. Complete Step 3 again for both sides.
5. Hold the center and open the wings out.

When the teacher says it's time for a practice flight, you will get a chance to see how effective your plane-making skills are. When you take your plane on its first flight, your observations will allow you to see what modifications might be necessary to result in a more efficient flight. Record your observations.

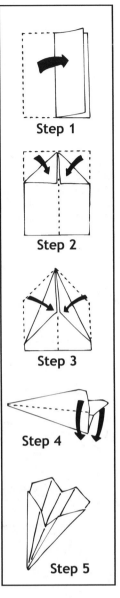

Step 1

Step 2

Step 3

Step 4

Step 5

_____

_____

_____

_____

TEAM CHALLENGE

Participants will work together in teams for a total of 12 minutes to make a paper airplane to be used for the flight contest. When the teacher signals it is time to stop working, teams will take their airplanes outside or into an open space for the contest.

The teacher will select groups of two or three for the team challenge and will assign a number to each group.

Once teams have been selected, the teacher will record the start time. You will have exactly 12 minutes to get your team's supplies and make your team's airplane. Any team that continues to work on its plane at any point after the teacher has called time may be disqualified from the contest. Your team's goal is to make a paper airplane that will travel the furthest distance.

Start Time _____ : _____ + 12 Minutes = _____ : _____ End Time

Airplanes must be released into flight at approximately 5 feet from the ground. When the teacher gives the signal, you will release your airplane and measure the distance from the start point. The goal is to have your team's plane complete the longest flight (in terms of distance, not time) from start to finish. Each team will have four flight opportunities. Distances must be recorded in the space provided.

1. Each team will take the best distance out of the four flight opportunities. Record the distances in the space below:

Flight #1 _____ yd _____ ft _____ in.   Flight #2 _____ yd _____ ft _____ in.

Flight #3 _____ yd _____ ft _____ in.   Flight #4 _____ yd _____ ft _____ in.

2. Convert each flight into inches. Remember that each yard = 36 inches, and each foot = 12 inches.

Flight #1 (_____ yd x 36 = _____ in.) + (_____ ft x 12 = _____ in.) + (_____ in.) = _____ total in.

Flight #2 (_____ yd x 36 = _____ in.) + (_____ ft x 12 = _____ in.) + (_____ in.) = _____ total in.

Flight #3 (_____ yd x 36 = _____ in.) + (_____ ft x 12 = _____ in.) + (_____ in.) = _____ total in.

Flight #4 (_____ yd x 36 = _____ in.) + (_____ ft x 12 = _____ in.) + (_____ in.) = _____ total in.

3. Compute the average inches traveled in a flight.

Flight #1 _____ in. + #2 _____ in. + #3 _____ in. + #4 _____ in. = total _____ in. ÷ 4 = _____ in.

4. What size would the paper be if it were doubled? _____ in. x _____ in.
Predict what might happen if the size of the plane were doubled. Explain your answer.

_____

_____

5. What size would the paper be if it were cut in half? _____ in. x _____ in.
Predict what might happen if the size of the plane were cut in half. Explain your answer.

_____

_____

6. What was the furthest distance traveled by an airplane in today's challenge? _____ in.

7. Convert this distance back into yards, feet, and inches. _____ in. = _____ yd _____ ft _____ in.

EXTEND THE LEARNING WITH AERODYNAMICS: PROJECT IDEAS

1. **Testing drag.** Drag, also known as air (or fluid) resistance, is a force that influences an object's movement through air or water. Understanding how drag can positively and/or negatively impact the way an object moves helps us to design objects for better efficiency. Test how drag influences the aerodynamics of ordinary objects, and see which objects will produce the most drag. Use several different types and sizes of objects. Some suggestions include the following:
   a. Spheres (e.g., baseball, grapefruit, orange)
   b. Rectangular shapes (e.g., cube, plastic block, box)
   c. Circular shapes (e.g., frisbee, plate, CD)
   d. Irregular shapes (e.g., toy, pipe, hammer, jar, boomerang)

   Write a page-long summary of what you found when you experimented with the drag of various objects in air and water. If it is useful to include sketches, please do so.

2. **Aerodynamic materials.** Once you've created a paper airplane, you can make other airplanes using a variety of materials to compare the aerodynamics. Some suggestions include newspaper, wrapping paper, cardboard, tag board, stock paper, Styrofoam, foil, and so on. Create an airplane out of some other material that improves upon your team's paper airplane. Write a paragraph explaining the improvements that you made and why they work.

3. **Wing design and lift.** The effectiveness of an airplane's wing design is important for the lift. Lift is the physical property that enables a plane to fly in the air. Test various wing designs to determine which provides the greatest amount of lift. First design wing shapes with various angles. Experiment to see if one design provides better lift. Add weights (paper clips, pennies, uncooked beans, and so on) to the wing to further experiment with lift. The more weight a wing can take, the more effective it is in terms of lift. Take a photo of each wing design you try, and write a few sentences explaining the effect of each design. Compile these into a photo report.

Hammock Among Us

Create a hammock to hold the most golf balls or other weight.

Subjects and Skills

- Estimation, analysis, prediction
- Using natural resources

Materials

- String or yarn
- Newspaper or fabric scraps
- Tape
- Straws or dowels

Vocabulary

- Hammock
- Sisal plants
- Indigenous

Purpose

Hammocks have been around for almost 1,000 years and are still in use today. Learning about the simple design of hammocks, as well as the natural materials traditionally used to create them, will help students better understand basic engineering principles.

Objectives

Students will:
- learn about the history of hammocks,
- understand how natural materials can serve as useful resources,
- analyze the potential flaws of the hammock's design, and
- provide ideas for solutions to these problems.

Activity Preparation

1. Run off activity sheets.
2. Gather materials and place them in two different areas in the room.
3. Bookmark websites to be used in class.
   a. http://www.hammocks.com/historyofhammocksarticle.cfm
   b. http://www.ecomall.com/greenshopping/hammock.htm

Activity Procedure

1. Students will independently read and highlight the information on the activity sheet, answer the questions, and sketch a hammock based on the reading.
2. Divide students into groups of two or three, and assign group numbers.
3. Ask students to share in their groups one new idea they learned. Ask groups then to share with the class what new things they learned.
4. Review the history of hammocks and the associated vocabulary.
5. Allow groups to settle and discuss plans for creating the hammock before beginning the challenge. Hold the challenge in whatever manner is easiest and most convenient for your classroom.
6. After the competition, have students complete the activity sheet.
7. If you wish, assign one of the projects suggested in Extend the Learning With Hammocks: Project Ideas.

Hammock Among Us

Name: _____   Date: _____

Hammock Among Us

GOAL

> Create a hammock to hold the most golf balls or other weight.

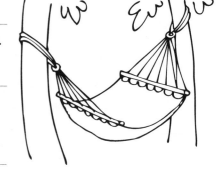

MATERIALS

> String or yarn
> Newspaper or fabric scraps
> Tape
> Straws or dowels

TIME TO CREATE

> 25 minutes

INDIVIDUAL ACTIVITY

Read the following and highlight the important information, and then respond to the questions.

> Hammock
> Pronunciation: **Ha**-muk
> Etymology: Spanish *hamaca*, from Taino
> Definition: A swinging bed usually made of netting and slung by cords at each end.

The hammock is used today by millions of people around the world. Although most people know about the hammock, some may not know where the hammock originated.

History books explain that the bark of the Hammock tree was used to weave the first hammock. The Sisal plant eventually replaced the bark, because Sisal plants were more abundant, and its fibers could be softened. A lot of clothing today is made from this same material.

Hammocks have been used by people in South America and Central America for almost 1,000 years. Hammocks were woven from indigenous fabrics and materials, meaning that people in different areas used the materials native to the area that were available to them; therefore, hammocks were made from a variety of materials, and in a variety of different styles.

By the 18th century, hammocks in North America were a novelty. Most hammocks were narrow, with wood staves, and required a bit of balance and skill on the part of those who sat and lay in them. In the 1880s, a wider hammock was created, and it became quite popular in North America.

1. What material are most hammocks made from today? _____

2. Define indigenous. _____

_____

3. On a separate sheet of paper, draw a sketch of what you think a hammock should look like.

TEAM CHALLENGE

Participants will work together in teams for a total of 25 minutes to design and build a hammock. The teacher will select groups of two or three for the team challenge and will assign a number to each group.

Start Time _____ : _____ + 25 Minutes = _____ : _____ End Time

On a separate sheet of paper, each member must draw a sketch of the agreed-upon team hammock. As a team, and using only the materials provided, build the hammock as closely in keeping with the plan as possible in 25 minutes. The dimensions of the hammock need to be larger than 7" x 7" but less than 11" x 11". The height of the hammock must be at least 6" off the base. Any shape is acceptable for your team's hammock. At some point in the 25 minutes, be sure to test your hammock with one golf ball and record your results in the space provided (Numbers 1 and 2), using your results to refine your hammock design.

1. Predict how many golf balls the hammock will be able to hold. _____
2. Try one golf ball and see what happens. Record your findings and what you learned from the one-golf-ball test. _____

_____

_____

When the teacher signals that it is time to stop working, take your team's hammock to the test site. Any team that continues to work after the stop time may be disqualified from the contest.

1. How many golf balls did your hammock hold?
2. If you were to rebuild the hammock, what would you do differently and why?

_____

_____

_____

3. Getting in and/or out of a hammock can be difficult for some people. How would you design a hammock that would make getting in and/or out easier?

_____

_____

_____

EXTEND THE LEARNING WITH HAMMOCKS: PROJECT IDEAS

1. **Selling the hammock lifestyle.** Create a commercial for a new and improved hammock. Be sure to provide factual information in an entertaining manner.

2. **Hammock H2O.** What modifications would need to be made if you were designing a hammock that would hold water? Write a one-page paper about how you would change your hammock to hold water, and provide a sketch.

3. **Hammocks and sports.** What athletic event could include a hammock as part of the event? Why or how? Write a script for a radio broadcast of this event describing how the hammock plays into the event.

4. **Slings.** The structure of the hammock is based on the shape of the sling. How do we use slings today? Research other ways in which the sling provides a purposeful use. Prepare a two-paragraph report on different ways we use slings.

Windmills on Your Mind?

Create two windmills and compare their rotation; make a windmill in which the rotation of the blades will continue the longest time with only the wind to help.

Subjects and Skills

- Wind as a natural resource, renewable resources
- Capacity, congruence, analysis

Materials

- Index cards
- Clay
- Paper cups
- Tape
- Metal brads
- Rulers
- Pencils
- Beads
- Paper
- An area outdoors in the wind where windmills can be tested, or an indoor fan

Vocabulary

- Energy forms (chemical, electrical, mechanical, solar, liquid, wind)
- Capacity
- Turbines
- Generators
- Congruent

Purpose

Learning how wind can be used as a powerful renewable resource is important for conservation. The understanding of how wind can create energy allows students to think about other ways in which wind might be used to replace non-renewable sources.

Objectives

Students will:
- understand how energy is created in various forms,
- focus on wind energy,
- gain a better understanding of the multiple ways in which we use wind energy, and

◆ design and create two different types of windmills to compare and analyze their energy output.

Activity Preparation

1. Run off activity sheets.
2. Gather materials and place them in two different areas in the room.
3. Bookmark websites to be used in class.
   a. http://www.clean-energy-ideas.com/resources/index.html   and/or http://www.brainpopjr.com/science/conservation
   b. http://www.energy.siemens.com/fi/en/energy-topics/videos/new-wind-turbine.htm
   c. http://vimeo.com/38203479
   d. http://news.bbc.co.uk/2/hi/8235456.stm

Activity Procedure

1. Discuss the differences between renewable and natural resources. The sun, the wind, tides, and geothermal activity are renewable and provide solar energy, wind energy, tidal energy, and geothermal energy, which help the environment.
2. Visit Link a. for information about energy-saving resources and ideas.
3. Discuss why and how we need to rely on different renewable, natural energy sources to help take the burden off of fossil fuels.
4. Distribute the activity sheets. Students will read and highlight information on the activity sheets. After they have read the information, show two videos: one on wind turbines (04:25), found at Link b., and another on the Palm Springs windmills (01:36), found at Link c. Discuss the videos with students.
5. Show the video on the world's first full-scale floating wind turbines (02:45), found at Link d.
6. The students will independently complete the activity sheets up until the team challenge section.
7. Put students into groups of three or four and assign a number to each group. Review the team challenge as necessary, answer any questions students may have, and start the timer.
8. After the allotted work time, the competition will begin. Hold the competition in the manner that best suits your classroom. You can take students outside to test their windmills in the breeze, or you can simply use an indoor fan.
9. Once the competition has ended, have students complete the activity sheet as they reflect upon and analyze the windmills.
10. If you wish, assign one of the activities suggested in Extend the Learning With Windmills: Web Activities.

Windmills on Your Mind?

GOAL

➢ Create two windmills and compare their rotation; make a windmill in which the rotation of the blades will continue the longest time with only the wind to help.

MATERIALS

➢ Index cards
➢ Clay
➢ Paper cups
➢ Tape
➢ Metal brads

➢ Rulers
➢ Pencils
➢ Beads
➢ Paper

TIME TO CREATE

➢ 25 minutes

INDIVIDUAL ACTIVITY

Read the following and highlight the important information. After a class discussion, provide responses to the questions.

What is energy? Energy is the capacity to do work and transfer heat. Work is performed when an object or substance is moved over some distance. Energy is needed for something to happen. Think about boiling water or a burning candle. Energy is the heat that flows from a hot object or substance to a cold object or substance when they come in contact.

Energy can be seen in many forms, such as light, heat, electricity, chemicals (stored in chemical bonds), and mechanical operations (in moving matter, such as flowing water). There are many sources in nature that provide energy. Remember that energy is the capacity to do work and transfer heat, which happens constantly in nature.

One such source of energy is wind. Turbine generators are a type of windmill that produce electricity by harnessing the wind. Wind turbine generators require average wind speeds of at least 21 km/h (13 mph). The largest of these windmills stands 150 ft tall with blades half the length of a football field. A wind turbine can produce 300 kilowatts an hour—the amount of electricity used by a typical household in a month. Almost all of the currently installed wind electric generation capacity occurs in California. The high-tech megatowers are engineered in cooperation with NASA and are taken care of by federal and state subsidies.

1. Provide an example of how we use some of this natural energy in our everyday lives.

_____

_____

Hands-On Engineering © Prufrock Press Inc.

Permission is granted to photocopy or reproduce this page for single classroom use only.

25

2. Besides fire, name another source in nature that provides heat. _____

3. Name a source in nature not named here that could provide energy. _____

_____

4. Hold up this sheet of paper and gently blow to observe the reaction. What would be the best shape and angle for a sail to catch and use the wind? (The sails are the blades of the windmill.) _____

5. Think about the design of a windmill. What are important elements for a windmill to have in order to rotate without much effort? _____

_____

TEAM CHALLENGE

Participants will work together in teams for a total of 25 minutes to make two different types of windmills: one that has sails attached to a base, and one that looks like a pinwheel. When the teacher signals that it is time to stop working, stop working immediately. Any team that continues to work after time has been called may be disqualified. The teacher will select groups of three or four and assign a number to each group. Once teams have been selected, the teacher will record the start time. You will have exactly 25 minutes to get your team's supplies and make your team's windmills according to the instructions below.

Start Time _____ : _____ + 25 Minutes = _____ : _____ End Time

1. For the first windmill, you will need to make a sail template to use for each sail. Decide what should be used as the hub (center) of the windmill to hold the sails. Each sail needs to be congruent. A cup can be used as the base or stand of the windmill. Make a small hole with a pencil in the center of a cup. The pencil could be used to hold the windmill. The sails need to move around the hub so that it spins easily. Gently blow on the windmill to observe what happens to the sails. Make any necessary adjustments.

2. Make the second windmill following these directions (see p. 27):
   a. Draw two diagonal lines so that they cross in the middle. Cut 2/3 of the way on each line towards the center.
   b. Bend the paper back along each cut line toward the center until you have all four corners folded into the center. Glue the corners.
   c. Push a brad through all four corners at the center. A small bead on the back might help with the rotation.
   d. Use the film container as a stabilizer.

When the teacher signals the time to stop working, take the windmills to the contest site. Any team that continues to work after the teacher has signaled the stop time may be disqualified.

1. Count the rotations for 15 seconds, and then multiply that number by 4 to get the number of rotations per full minute.

    a. Windmill #1: _____ rotations per minute

    b. Windmill #2: _____ rotations per minute

2. Compare the two windmills. Which has the better rotation?

    _____

    _____

3. What was the most significant difference between the two windmills?

    _____

    _____

    _____

    _____

4. What factors contributed to the success of the more effective windmill?

    _____

    _____

    _____

    _____

5. How might you use a windmill at your home as a source of energy?

    _____

    _____

    _____

    _____

Step 1

Step 2

Step 3

Step 4

Step 5

EXTEND THE LEARNING WITH WINDMILLS: WEB ACTIVITIES

1. **Energy production WebQuest.** Go on an exciting educational WebQuest to learn more about energy production and think about alternative ways to conserve energy. Visit http://www.energyquest.ca.gov.

2. **Energy engineering WebQuest.** You are an energy engineer employed by Energy Quest Incorporated, and you and a team have been hired by Power City to determine which forms of energy the city should use to produce electricity. The city council wants to use one renewable energy form and one nonrenewable energy form to produce the city's electrical power. Work in a team of other student energy engineers to determine the best forms of energy for this city to use. Visit http://www.catawba.k12.nc.us/techtrac/plus/muckinhoupt.

3. **Energy process WebQuest.** You will take on a specific role (energy expert, analyst, environmental expert, conservationist expert) and analyze energy sources. Visit http://nanunet.lhric.org/AMBarrMiddleSchool/insttech/energywq/EnergyWQSProcess.htm.

4. **Alternative fuels WebQuest.** You will analyze alternative fuels and discover how the use of such fuels can reduce overall air pollution from vehicles. Different types of alternative fuels will be analyzed in order to identify which appear to be most cost effective. You will also learn about other energy sources that can be used to power vehicles. Visit http://www.glencoe.com/sec/science/webquest/content/altfuels.shtml.

5. **Energy resources tutorial.** Learn about fossil fuels, nuclear power, solar power, wind power, tidal power, hydroelectric power, pumped storage, wave power, geothermal power, and biofuels. Each topic has engaging resource activities that you might complete. Visit http://www.darvill.clara.net/altenerg.

Will It Go Round in Circles?

Make the closest estimate of the area and circumference of the circle created by the team members sitting cross-legged.

Subjects and Skills

- Geometry
- Estimating measurement, converting units of measurement
- Circles (circumference, diameter, area, pi)

Materials

- String or yarn
- Metersticks/yardsticks (use only after team challenge has been completed)
- Calculators

Vocabulary

- Cubits
- Digit
- Span
- Fathom
- Circumference

- Diameter
- Pi
- Radius
- Area

Purpose

The concepts associated with circles are based on fundamental geometric principles. Students will create their own circles and will understand what the circumference and area look like, as well as how they are related to circles.

Objectives

Students will:
- estimate the area and circumference of a circle;
- check estimation by finding the exact measurements;

- relate area and circumference to real life as they physically form a circle with their group;
- define diameter, radius, pi, area, and circumference; and
- understand how measurements have changed over time.

Activity Preparation

1. Run off activity sheets.
2. Gather materials and place them in two different areas in the room.
3. Bookmark websites to be used in class.
   a. http://www.touregypt.net/featurestories/measures.htm
   b. http://boatsafe.com/tools/meter.htm

Activity Procedure

1. Ask students to think about how specific measurements originated. Why did people develop measurements? What did they use for measuring? What purpose did people have for specifically defining measurements?
2. Share information from Link a. about the weights and measures of Ancient Egypt.
3. Write and discuss the vocabulary related to measurement, specifically area and circumference of circles.
4. Have students read and complete Questions 1–9 on the activity sheet. In this series of questions, students estimate measurements of lengths in the classroom. They can do this individually, or you can conduct the activity as a whole class. It is up to you whether or not to provide actual measurements (or allow students to measure the actual lengths themselves), although it is not necessary. When teaching fathom conversion, you might go to Link b. for helpful information.
5. While students are working independently on the practice problems (Question 10), put students into groups of four or five, and assign group numbers.
6. Review the answers to Question 10 (a. 9.42 cm; b. 8.4 in.; c. 12.56 yd; d. 3 m).
7. Review the team challenge, answer any questions students may have, and start the clock for the team challenge.
8. After the challenge has been completed, have students complete the rest of the activity sheet. Teams will check each other's calculations (based on estimations), and then students will measure and calculate the actual dimensions and area of their circles.
9. If you wish, assign one of the activities suggested in Extend the Learning With Circles: Websites and Activities.

Will It Go Round in Circles?

GOAL

➢ Make the closest estimate of the area and circumference of the circle created by the team members sitting cross-legged.

MATERIALS

➢ String or yarn
➢ Metersticks/yardsticks (use only after team challenge has been completed)
➢ Calculators

TIME FOR ACTIVITY

➢ 12 minutes

INDIVIDUAL ACTIVITY

1. Before technology had been designed to help gauge accurate measurements, people used handy instruments—literally. For example, the width of an index finger became a *digit*. How many digits wide is your desk? _____

2. The length of the arm from the tip of the middle finger to the elbow became a *cubit*. From your seat, estimate how many cubits tall you think the class doorway might be: _____

3. The Romans used the length of a grown man's foot as a measurement tool. What do you think that unit of measurement was named? _____ How many inches long do you think your foot is? _____

4. What besides a ruler might be used to measure an inch? _____

5. The width of the outstretched hand from the thumb to the little finger was called a *span*. Approximately how many spans wide is your desk? _____

6. The length from fingertip to fingertip with arms outstretched is a *fathom*. Using fathoms, what do you think your classroom's length and width are? _____

7. Leonardo da Vinci used a *braccio*, or arm's length, when planning his work. A braccio was equal to two *palmi*, or outstretched palms. Approximately how many braccio in height are you? _____

8. Around 250 B.C., the Greek mathematician Archimedes figured out the ratio of a circle's circumference to its diameter. What is the formula for measuring circumference? _____ What is the formula for measuring area? _____

9. What is the value of pi? _____

10. Practice on your own with these problems:

    a. The diameter of a nickel is 3 cm. What is the circumference? _____

    b. The radius of a plate is 4.2 in. What is the diameter? _____

    c. The radius of a circular rug is 2 yd. What is the area? _____

    d. The circumference of a wheel is 18.84 m. What is the radius? _____

TEAM CHALLENGE

Participants will work in teams of four or five to form a circle and make estimates and calculations based on that circle's measurements. Once teams have been selected, the teacher will record the start time. You will have exactly 12 minutes to get your supplies and make your team's circle. Your goal is make a circle and be the closest with your estimations/calculations of the diameter, circumference, and area. You will record your estimates in the box provided.

Start Time _____ : _____ + 12 Minutes = _____ : _____ End Time

Sit cross-legged as closely together as possible in a circle, and use the yarn or string provided to outline the group circle. Estimate what the circle's diameter might be. Calculate the circumference and the area based on this estimate. Don't forget to include the units on all measurements. Leave the yarn outline of your circle in place until the end of the challenge.

ESTIMATIONS OF MEASUREMENTS

1. Our estimate of the diameter: _____

2. Our estimate of the circumference: _____

3. Our estimate of the area: _____

When the time period is up, pass your paper to another team to check the accuracy of your group's calculations. Use a calculator and pen and write neatly when checking another team's work.

The team that is checking the measurements recorded in the box should complete the following:

Based on the estimated measurement of the team's diameter equaling _____, the

circumference equals _____ and the area equals _____. The team's calculations were

(circle one) correct/ incorrect.

If one or more of the team's calculations was incorrect, write in the space provided where you think the team's error took place.

_____

_____

_____

_____

_____

_____

_____

_____

_____

_____

Each team should now get its checked calculations back from the team that checked them. It is now time to check for accuracy of estimation by using a yard- or meterstick.

1. Measure the diameter of your group's circle and record the information below.

   Diameter = _____ Circumference = _____ Area = _____

2. What was the difference between your estimation and the actual measurement?

   Diameter = _____ Circumference = _____ Area = _____

3. Were you successful in estimating the diameter? _____

4. Were you successful calculating the circumference? _____ The area? _____

5. How could your team have been more accurate? _____

   _____

6. Sometimes estimating measurements is sufficient, and sometimes we need to be precise.

   Give two examples of when estimation is sufficient. _____

   _____

   Give two examples of when measurements must be precise. _____

   _____

7. Why is it important to understand measurement? _____

   _____

EXTEND THE LEARNING WITH CIRCLES: WEBSITES AND ACTIVITIES

1. **Interactive circle.** Learn the concepts of chords, tangents, and circular sectors. Visit http://www.misterteacher.com/everything_geometry/interactivecircle.html.

2. **Circle tool.** Investigate the relationships of area and circumference of a circle compared to its radius and diameter. Visit http://illuminations.nctm.org/ActivityDetail.aspx?ID=116.

3. **Computing pi.** Explore how Archimedes approximated pi by using polygons and calculating perimeters. Visit http://illuminations.nctm.org/ActivityDetail.aspx?ID=161.

4. **Linking circles to cylinders.** The volume of a cylinder is calculated by multiplying the area of the circle base of a cylinder by the height of the cylinder: $V = \pi r^2 h$. Gather various cylindrical objects, such as cans, and record the diameter of the top of each cylindrical object. Use this information to find, for each object, the radius of the circular base, the area of the circular base, the height of the cylinder, and the volume of the cylinder. Make a table containing this information.

Building Bridges

Build a sturdy bridge with a 2-foot span that can be transported from one spot to another.

Subjects and Skills
- Fundamental principles of engineering
- Various bridge designs

Materials Needed
- Index cards
- Paper
- Rulers
- Pennies
- Straws
- Self-adhesive labels
- Toothpicks
- Bridge test site (two stacks of books of equal height 2 feet apart)

Vocabulary
- Beam bridge
- Suspension bridge
- Anchorage

Purpose
Students can appreciate the engineering and design of bridges by understanding the physical laws and fundamental principles that guide the development and application of bridge conception and construction.

Objectives
Students will:
- understand the fundamental principles necessary in the development of bridges,
- analyze engineering of different types of bridges, and
- design and build a bridge.

Activity Preparation
1. Run off activity sheets.
2. Gather materials and place them in two different areas of the room.
3. Bookmark websites to be used in class.
   a. http://videos.howstuffworks.com/tlc/28828-understanding-history-of-bridge-construction-video.htm

Building Bridges

b. http://videos.howstuffworks.com/tlc/29830-understanding-bridge-movement-video.htm
c. http://videos.howstuffworks.com/tlc/29829-understanding-bridge-designs-video.htm
d. http://videos.howstuffworks.com/discovery/35894-howstuffworks-show-episode-12-steel-bridges-video.htm
e. http://dsc.discovery.com/videos/we-built-this-city-new-york-the-brooklyn-bridge.html
f. http://www.pbs.org/wgbh/buildingbig/bridge/basics.html
g. http://www.brantacan.co.uk/bridges.htm

Activity Procedure

1. Begin the class discussion with the following questions: What types of bridges do we use today? What purposes do they serve? How are they made?
2. Watch some or all of the following videos online:
   a. Link a., History of Bridge Construction (02:41)
   b. Link b., Bridge Movement (01:28)
   c. Link c., Bridge Designs (02:08)
   d. Link d., Steel Bridges (02:54)
   e. Link e., The Brooklyn Bridge (01:55)

3. Share information found at two excellent sites on bridge basics, found at Link f. and Link g.
4. Summarize the video and website information. You could do this as a class, in partners, or in small groups, and you should use your method of choice for review (e.g., calling on students, writing paragraphs or questions).
5. Distribute the activity sheet to continue the discussion.
6. Have students highlight information and use what they have learned to draw sketches of the five different types of bridges.
7. While students are working on the individual section of the activity sheet, put students in small groups of three or four students and assign group numbers.
8. After students have used the allotted time to construct their bridges, begin the competition. It works well to erect two stacks of books of equal height 2 feet apart so that students can move their bridges to this test site and load their bridge with pennies.
9. After the competition, have students evaluate the construction and design of their bridges, and discuss the elements of the different bridges.
10. If you wish, assign one of the activities in Extend the Learning With Bridges: Activities.

Building Bridges

GOAL

- ➤ Build a sturdy bridge with a 2-foot span that can be transported from one spot to another.

MATERIALS

- ➤ Index cards
- ➤ Paper
- ➤ Ruler
- ➤ Pennies
- ➤ Straws
- ➤ Self-adhesive labels
- ➤ Toothpicks

TIME TO CREATE

- ➤ 20 minutes

INDIVIDUAL ACTIVITY

There are five types of bridges. Read the information about the different types of bridges, and draw a sketch of what each might look like.

A beam bridge is the simplest kind of bridge. A log that has fallen across a river or a board lain across a puddle forms a beam bridge.

SKETCH OF BEAM BRIDGE

Hands-On Engineering © Prufrock Press Inc.   37

Permission is granted to photocopy or reproduce this page for single classroom use only.

Arches have been common features in structures since 1,000 B.C., but they didn't appear in bridges for another thousand years. Roman roads were often supported by stone arches.

SKETCH OF ARCHES

Suspension bridges, like the Golden Gate Bridge, rely on cables for their support. Each cable end must be anchored to a massive block of concrete called an anchorage. The cable pulls on the anchorages.

SKETCH OF SUSPENSION BRIDGE

Cantilever bridges are supported by cantilevers, which are beams, or structural frameworks, that are fixed at one end and free at the other, much like diving boards. Most of the flexing, or bending, takes place in the middle of a cantilever bridge; therefore, the deepest part should be at the middle.

SKETCH OF CANTILEVER BRIDGE

Cable-stayed bridges are supported by a series of cables. Each forms the leg of a triangle and extends from a tower or towers. Cable-stays are straight and anchor directly into the roadway.

SKETCH OF CABLE-STAYED BRIDGES

Think about the following questions on your own before designing and building a bridge with your team.

1. What kind of bridge do you think would be the sturdiest? _____

   Why? _____

   _____

2. Which bridge would be the easiest to make? _____

   Why? _____

   _____

3. How could you change an index card and/or regular paper to make it sturdier?

_____

_____

_____

4. How might folding paper into pleats (like a fan) make paper stronger?

_____

_____

_____

TEAM CHALLENGE

Participants will work in small teams to design and build a bridge in 20 minutes. The bridge must have a 2-foot span and be able to be moved from one designated location to another without falling apart. You want your bridge to hold the most weight before collapsing. First draw the plan of the bridge to scale. Use one sheet of paper per team for the design, and label everything. Once the design is complete, begin constructing the bridge. Once the teacher has called time, stop working immediately. Any team that continues to work after time has been called may be disqualified.

Start Time _____ : _____ + 20 Minutes = _____ : _____ End Time

Before your group begins designing your bridge, think about the following questions:

1. What kind of bridge do you plan on making? _____

2. Explain why you decided on that type of bridge. _____

_____

_____

3. Draw a sketch of your team's bridge.

4. Which of the available materials will you need to make this bridge? _____

_____

_____

After your bridge has been constructed, answer the following questions:

5. A roll of 50 pennies weighs 132 grams, which is a about 4.5 ounces. How many ounces are in a pound? _____

6. Approximately how many pennies would weigh 1 pound? _____

7. How many pennies do you think you can pile on your bridge before it collapses? _____

When the teacher signals that it is time to stop working, take the bridges to the test site. After the contest, answer the following questions:

1. How many pennies was your bridge able to hold before it collapsed? _____

2. What is the class record of pennies a team's bridge was able to hold today? _____

3. What contributed to the success of the bridge with the class record?

_____

_____

Hands-On Engineering © Prufrock Press Inc.

Permission is granted to photocopy or reproduce this page for single classroom use only.

41

EXTEND THE LEARNING WITH BRIDGES: ACTIVITIES

1. **Bridges for the future.** The United States has more than 76,000 bridges. Technology today is more advanced and allows us to utilize unique methods for building smarter bridges. Visit http://www.pbs.org/wgbh/nova/tech/bridge-collapse.html to read about why some have failed. Design and draw a bridge for the future.

2. **Bridge projects.** Visit http://bridgepros.com/projects/index.html and investigate one of the bridge projects listed there. Write a paragraph explaining this project.

3. **Tacoma bridge collapse of 1940.** Visit http://bridgecontest.phys.iit.edu/public/help for a lecture and tutorial about this event. Skip ahead to minute 10:58 to watch the swaying of the bridge prior to its collapse. Write a paragraph explaining the reasons for the collapse and how such accidents are prevented now.

4. **Labs for understanding forces, materials, loads, and shapes.** Choose from among the following labs:
   - Complete the forces lab found at http://www.pbs.org/wgbh/buildingbig/lab/forces.html, which demonstrates real-life forces that affect structures and teaches about different forces that a bridge experiences.
   - Complete the materials lab at http://www.pbs.org/wgbh/buildingbig/lab/materials.html, which demonstrates the different materials used to build structures.
   - Complete the loads lab found at http://www.pbs.org/wgbh/buildingbig/lab/loads.html, which demonstrates the forces, or loads, that act on the structures.
   - Complete the shapes lab found at http://www.pbs.org/wgbh/buildingbig/lab/shapes.html, which demonstrates how the shapes of structures affect their strength.

5. **Build a bridge.** Complete one of the following build-a-bridge activities:
   - Interactive bridge: http://www.pbs.org/wgbh/nova/bridge
   - Spaghetti bridge: http://civil.camosun.bc.ca/spaghetti_bridge/Tips.htm
   - PBS bridge challenge: http://www.pbs.org/wgbh/buildingbig/bridge/challenge/index.html
   - Suspension bridge: http://www.pbs.org/wgbh/buildingbig/educator/act_suspension_ho.html

It's All Downhill From Here

Create the fastest rolling object with a 5" diameter that will travel down a 6' incline.

Subjects and Skills

- Geometry of circles and cylinders
- Calculating surface area
- Kinetic energy, velocity, acceleration
- Mass, law of gravity

Materials

- Paper
- Straws
- Tape
- Rulers
- Timers with stop/start buttons
- Incline of 6' (e.g., a plank leaned against a desk, a slide)
- Rubber band

Vocabulary

- Circumference
- Pi
- Cylinder
- Surface area
- Kinetic energy
- Velocity
- Acceleration
- Inclined plane
- Mass
- Gravity

Purpose

An understanding of the core concepts of mechanical energy, either as kinetic energy (energy of motion) or potential energy (stored energy of position), is the foundation of mechanical engineering. The physics of mechanical energy play a significant role in everything we do.

Objectives

Students will:
- understand how kinetic energy and potential energy relate to motion;

- apply previously learned mathematic concepts, such as circumference and area of circles, as they learn how mass and speed play an important role in the movement of an object;
- discover how kinetic energy can be transferred in different ways; and
- understand how kinetic energy can be transformed into electricity.

Activity Preparation

1. Run off activity sheets.
2. Gather materials and place them in two separate areas of the room. Be sure that you have an incline that will work for all students to use, such as a plank propped against a desk. This incline should be around 6' long.
3. Bookmark websites to be used in class.
   a. http://www.teachertube.com/viewVideo.php?video_id=127812
   b. http://tinyurl.com/28mxzf6
   c. http://www.teachertube.com/viewVideo.php?video_id=53066

Activity Procedure

1. Write "Kinetic Energy" and "Potential Energy" on the board. Ask students to share what they know about both types of energy.
2. Stretch a rubber band and hold it in the "ready" position, but do not let go. The stretch demonstrates potential energy. Aim the rubber band at a wall, and discuss how potential energy is converted to kinetic energy as you launch it at the wall.
3. Drop an object from the top of a desk. Throw an object across the room. Ask, "What types of energy were being used in these objects' movements?"
4. Discuss that the amount of kinetic energy depends upon the mass and speed of the object. Mass refers to how much matter is within an object. All objects and materials have mass.
5. Allow 5 minutes for students to work with a partner to explain their understanding of mass and the differences between kinetic and potential energy.
6. Share the video (3:55) on kinetic and potential energy found at Link a.
7. Pass out the activity sheet, and explain that students will be applying their understanding of energy in today's challenge.
8. Play the energy song at Link b. or show the video with lyrics (01:59) at Link c.
9. Have students complete the individual portion of the activity sheet. Divide students into small groups of two or three students each, and assign a number to each team.

10. Review the challenge with students and answer any questions they may have.

11. Conduct the challenge. If possible, you may choose to have teams race their rollers two at a time, rather than timing the rollers on an individual basis. This makes things a bit more exciting, as the students are watching the rollers compete one on one. The number of timers you use, as well as who does the timing, are up to you—things can get a bit contentious if more than one person is timing a race, but if somebody is timing and makes an error, the students may get upset. Thus, it may be best if you time all of the races or if there are designated timers.

12. After the challenge, discuss the results with students and have them complete their activity sheets.

13. If you wish, assign one of the activities suggested in Extend the Learning With Kinetic Energy: Online Resources and Activities.

It's All Downhill From Here

GOAL

➢ Create the fastest rolling object with a 5" diameter that will travel down a 6' incline.

MATERIALS

➢ Paper   ➢ Tape
➢ Straws   ➢ Rulers

TIME TO CREATE

➢ 15 minutes

INDIVIDUAL ACTIVITY

Read the following information and respond to the questions.

When you ride your bike down a hill, it's easy to go fast. Gravity is handling the work, so you don't have to exert much energy. The length and steepness of the hill can increase your speed—the steeper and longer the hill, the faster you go. The distribution of your mass and the incline of the slope will also affect the speed of movement.

When describing the motion of objects, we're actually describing kinetic energy, energy characterized by the movement of an object. Understanding kinetic energy helps us to use natural forces and/or create machines to improve the quality of our lives.

You will apply your understanding of kinetic energy in today's team challenge. However, before you begin the challenge, you'll need to refresh your memory on some geometric principles.

1. Define circumference. _____

2. What is half of a diameter called?_____

3. What is the value of pi? _____

4. To find the circumference of a circle, multiply pi by the: _____

5. What is the formula to find the area of a circle? _____

6. Find the circumference and area of a circle with a 3-inch radius. _____

7. Define surface area._____

8. What is the formula for finding the surface area of a cylinder? _____

9. Imagine taking apart the cylinder on the following page. You would have the top, bottom, and middle. This is called a net. Think about the shapes of each part. Draw the net and include the measurements for the radius on the top and bottom, and the length and width of the middle.

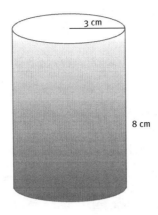

3 cm

8 cm

10. Find the area of the: top: _____ bottom: _____ middle: _____

11. What is the surface area of this cylinder? _____

12. What is the formula for finding the volume (inside area) of a cylinder? _____

13. Use this formula to find the volume of the cylinder in Question 9. _____

TEAM CHALLENGE

Participants will work in teams of two or three to create a rolling object with a 5" diameter within an allotted time of 15 minutes. A 6' slope of approximately 45 degrees will be provided by the teacher, and all of the teams will use this slope. The goal is to have the roller that travels the fastest down this slope.

Start Time _____ : _____ + 15 Minutes = _____ : _____ End Time

1. For each race, record the times of each team's rollers. Find the sum of each column.

Roller #1: _____ : _____   Roller #2: _____ : _____   Roller #3: _____ : _____

Roller #4: _____ : _____   Roller #5: _____ : _____   Roller #6: _____ : _____

Roller #7: _____ : _____   Roller #8: _____ : _____   Roller #9: _____ : _____

Roller #10: _____ : _____   Roller #11: _____ : _____   Roller #12: _____ : _____

Roller #13: _____ : _____   Roller #14: _____ : _____   Roller #15: _____ : _____

Column sums: _____ : _____   _____ : _____   _____ : _____

2. Using the column sums, compute the average of all rollers. Show your work.

Average time: _____ : _____

3. What do you think contributed to one roller being faster than another? Support your ideas.

_____

_____

_____

_____

_____

4. If you were to create the roller again, what would you do differently and why?

_____

_____

_____

_____

_____

5. In what real-life situations might this information be useful?

_____

_____

_____

_____

_____

EXTEND THE LEARNING WITH KINETIC ENERGY: ONLINE RESOURCES AND ACTIVITIES

1. **Design a roller coaster.** Visit one of the following sites to design your own roller coaster:
   - http://www.learner.org/interactives/parkphysics/coaster
   - http://dsc.discovery.com/games/coasters/interactive.html
   - http://sci-quest.org/learn/just-for-kids/build-roller-coaster
   - http://www.questacon.edu.au/indepth/maketracks/maketracks.html
   - http://www.funderstanding.com/coaster
   - http://puzzling.caret.cam.ac.uk/game.php?game=roller
   - http://www.dgp.toronto.edu/~lockwood/coaster/coaster.htm

2. **EdHeads resources.** Visit the EdHeads glossary and complete the lever lesson, and then play the game and go on the WebQuest.
   - Glossary: http://www.edheads.org/activities/simple-machines/glossary.htm
   - Lever lesson: http://www.edheads.org/activities/lesson_plans/pdf/sm_03.pdf
   - Game: http://www.edheads.org/activities/simple-machines/index.htm
   - WebQuest: http://www.edheads.org/activities/lesson_plans/pdf/sm_04.pdf

3. **Review games.** Visit the following Disney sites to play games that review kinetic and potential energy:
   - Rat 'n' Roll Pinball: http://www.disney--games.com/rat_n_roll_pinball_63.html
   - Disney Friends Golf: http://www.disney--games.com/disney_friends_golf_145.html
   - Disney Baseball: http://www.disney--games.com/disney_baseball_197.html

Cow-a-Bungee

Create a bungee jump (from the top of a bookshelf or tall cabinet) whose object has the most caroms from one jump.

Subjects and Skills

- Graphing lines using x- and y-axes (plotting coordinate points on a graph, slope, y-intercepts, creating a function)
- Kinetic energy, potential energy, gravity, rebound, carom

Materials

- Rubber bands
- Tape
- Rulers
- Graph paper

- Plastic animal (preferably a cow) or other "bungee jumper" object
- Bungee jumping site (bookshelf or other tall object)

Vocabulary

- Slipknot
- Bungee
- Potential energy
- Kinetic energy
- Gravity
- Carom

- Rebound
- Synthetic
- Slope
- x-axis
- y-axis
- y-intercept

Purpose

Applying statistics and algebraic functions to gain an understanding of the relationship between elasticity and energy will give students a better understanding of mathematical principles.

Objectives

Students will:
- determine the number of rubber bands needed to allow an object to bungee,
- plot coordinate points on a graph,

◆ learn the basic concepts of slope and y-intercepts,

◆ create a function, and

◆ solve equations to make predictions.

Activity Preparation

1. Run off activity sheets.
2. Gather materials and place them in two different areas of the room.
3. Bookmark websites to be used in class.
   a. http://www.iwillknot.com and/or http://www.wikihow.com/Make-a-Slip-Knot
   b. http://encyclopedia.kids.net.au/page/ho/Hooke's_law
   c. http://inventors.about.com/cs/inventorsalphabet/a/rubber_2.htm
   d. http://teachertube.com/viewVideo.php?title=Barbie_Bungee &video_id=198832
   e. http://www.metacafe.com/watch/46124/bungee_jumping_in_ new_zealand

Activity Procedure

1. Hold up a rubber band and ask the students to brainstorm its possible uses.
2. Demonstrate how the rubber band is able to move by being stretched and released.
3. Distribute rubber bands to students to practice slipknots. Teach students to make a slipknot with Link a. and/or the instructions on the activity sheet. Continue the discussion of rubber bands.
4. Review the concepts of kinetic and potential energy.
5. Distribute graph paper to introduce or review the terms/concepts of x-axis, y-axis, y-intercept, and slope. You can discuss these as simple concepts: The x-axis is the horizontal line; the y-axis is the vertical line; the y-intercept is the exact pair of coordinate points at which a line crosses over the y-axis; the slope is the steepness of a line from one coordinate point to another.
6. Optional: Introduce Hooke's law of elasticity (this states that the extension of a spring is in direct proportion with the load applied to it). For more information, visit Link b.
7. Discuss information on the history of rubber and/or synthetic elastic from Link c.
8. Show the images that come up when you run an image search for the phrase "bungee jumping." Show the video (01:27) of Barbie bungee jumping at Link d. You may also show a video (01:51) at Link e. of the

Cow-a-Bungee

jump from Kawarau Suspension Bridge, the site where bungee jumping gained popularity in 1988.

9. Put students into small groups, and assign group numbers.

10. Discuss the activity sheet and the team challenge, addressing any questions that students may have.

11. Students will collect data using bungee cords of varying lengths of rubber bands that will allow an object to fall as close as possible to the ground without hitting it. As each drop occurs, students record and graph their data, and then conduct an analysis to determine the linear equation. This may work best if you have numerous challenge sites of the same height in order to save time. Also, all teams should use the same object or objects of standard weight in order to make the challenge fair.

12. Have students complete their activity sheets once the challenge is completed. If students are ready, introduce and/or review the concepts of slope and y-intercept. Discuss the relationship between the graph and the experiment.

13. If you wish, assign one of the activities suggested in Extend the Learning With Bungee Jumping: Activities.

Cow-a-Bungee

GOAL

➢ Create a bungee jump (from the top of a bookshelf or tall cabinet) whose object has the most caroms from one jump.

MATERIALS

➢ Rubber bands
➢ Tape
➢ Rulers
➢ Graph paper

TIME TO CREATE

➢ 20 minutes

INDIVIDUAL ACTIVITY

Read the following information, highlighting key terms and ideas, and complete the activities.

The word bungee means "thick and squat." Bungee jumping originated on the Pacific island of Pentecost as a ritual. For centuries, the native men tested their manhood by jumping from tall bamboo towers, approximately 20–30 meters (260–400 yards), with vines tied to their ankles. Bungee jumping arrived in the United States in 1979 when members of the Oxford University Dangerous Sports Club jumped from the Golden Gate Bridge on elastic latex cords.

The height of the bungee above the ground creates a certain amount of potential energy. When the jumper jumps off, this potential energy is converted into kinetic energy and will continue to increase the speed during the fall. The bungee cord will kick in during the carom, or rebound, process and will begin transforming the kinetic and potential energy to elastic energy, which is stored in the cord and is the reason it stretches. Once the bungee stops, most of the potential energy and all of the kinetic energy have been converted to elastic energy.

You may already know that a rubber band is an elastic loop of natural or synthetic rubber used to hold objects together. But did you know that the use of rubber has been around for thousands of years? The Olmecs, a pre-Columbian civilization in South America, utilized the natural latex from the Hevea tree around 1500 B.C. Later, the Mayan people used this latex, or rubber, for various purposes. Latex, the sap of certain plants—specifically, the rubber tree—when exposed to the air, hardens and become rubbery. The rubber band was not officially invented until 1845, when a man by the name of Stephen Perry invented the rubber band to hold papers and envelopes together.

Hands-On Engineering © Prufrock Press Inc.

53

Permission is granted to photocopy or reproduce this page for single classroom use only.

Today, we use both natural and synthetic rubber. Natural rubber is the latex that is extracted from rubber trees, similar to how the Mayans accessed rubber. Synthetic rubber is made from refining byproducts of petroleum. Most of the rubber produced today is synthetic.

Place a rubber band on your desk and draw its relaxed shape in the space provided.

Name two different ways we use rubber today.

1. _____

_____

2. _____

_____

Continue to practice making a slipknot with your rubber band. If you need a reminder about how to make a slipknot, here are some illustrations:

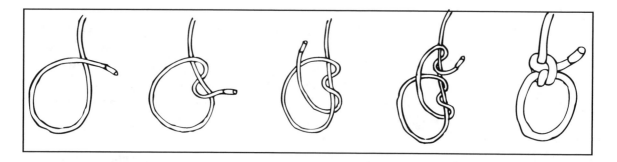

TEAM CHALLENGE

Participants will work in teams of two or three to create a bungee jump for a plastic animal (or a substitute object). The bungee must be designed for the participant (object) to safely bungee from the top of a typical bookshelf or tall structure. No part of the participating bungee-jumper (object) may touch the ground, and neither can it touch any other object (e.g., bookshelf), during the bungee process. The participant must carom (rebound) at least once; however, the challenge is for your bungee to have the most caroms.

The teacher will select groups of two or three for the team challenge and will assign a number to each group. Once teams have been selected, the teacher will record the start time. You will have exactly 20 minutes to get your supplies, make your team's bungee, and record the information. Your goal is to make a bungee jump from the top of a bookshelf or tall cabinet and to have the most caroms from one bungee jump.

A designated plastic participant must carom at least once and must not touch any object or the ground throughout the process.

Start Time _____:_____ + 20 Minutes = _____:_____ End Time

1. Attach a rubber band to the participant (object) by creating a slipknot, or double loop, to wrap around the object. Securing one rubber band to another with a slipknot will create a double loop.

2. Continue to attach more rubber bands to the first one in order to lengthen the cord. Measure the distance the object falls on the first drop. Repeat the jump two more times and record the distance.

Number of Rubber Bands	3	5	7
Distance in Inches			
Number of Caroms			

3. What is the average for the distance of the three jumps? _____

4. Continue adding rubber bands and measuring the distances. Use graph paper to plot the information. Label the x-axis as Number of Rubber Bands Used, and the y-axis as Distance in Inches.

5. Connect the points.

6. Predict the distance of the drop if you were to use 100 rubber bands. How did you get this prediction? _____

7. Express the equation for how to predict the distance of the drop (y) from how many rubber bands are used (x). _____

8. What is the slope of your equation? _____

9. What is the y-intercept of your equation? _____

10. How many rubber bands did you need for the participant to have a successful bungee? _____

11. What could be done to improve your team's bungee? _____

EXTEND THE LEARNING WITH BUNGEE JUMPING: ACTIVITIES

1. **Effects of gravity.** Consider the effects of gravity, and consider the speed at which a bungee participant falls during the jump. What is the speed 1 second after the jump starts? What is the speed at the bottom of the jump? Do research so that you can write a paragraph about how gravity affects the speed of a jump.

2. **Bungee jumping in reverse.** How do you apply the concepts we have already learned when thinking about bungee jumping in reverse? Review the video at http://www.snotr.com/video/1022 and write a paragraph about the differences in speed, elasticity, distance of carom, and so on.

3. **Bungee evolution.** Bungee jumping has evolved so that there are now many ways for thrill seekers to get their adrenaline fix: There is horizontal bungee jumping, reverse bungee jumping, and more. Using the concepts we've learned about, think of another way bungee jumping could evolve. Draw a picture of your new sport, labeling the parts of the picture and providing written explanation where necessary.

4. **Hooke's law of elasticity.** Research Hooke's law online. Make a list of the ways this law is useful to engineers and designers, including potential applications.

5. **Bungee interactive games.** Visit one of the following sites to play an interactive bungee game:
   - Bungee Rescue: http://www.freeworldgroup.com/games6/gameindex/bungee-rescue.htm
   - Bungee Bandit: http://www.newgrounds.com/portal/view/260318

6. **Experiment on stress of elastic limit.** Stress is an applied force that causes a material to be deformed (bent out of shape). Elastic materials are able to return to their original shape after being deformed, but even a rubber band has an elastic limit. If the rubber band is stretched too much, it doesn't return to its original shape. The elastic limit of a material is the maximum force on a material that results in the material returning to its original shape after the force is removed. Any stress less than the elastic limit will result in the material returning to its original shape. Any stress greater than the elastic limit will result in the material not returning to its original shape. Study the effects of the elastic limit on different-sized rubber bands, balloons, gummy worms, and other elastic items. Decide the stress limits in relationship to the item's elastic limit. Using a ruler, record the length of the object before the stress was applied, and at its furthest stretch mark. Experiment with five objects and record your results.

Stealthy Design

Create a stealth aircraft that will travel the furthest distance.

Subjects and Skills

- Measurement to the nearest eighth of an inch, calculating averages
- Radar's military uses, history of stealth planes

Materials

- 8.5" x 11" paper
- Metersticks or yardsticks
- A challenge site for students to fly stealth planes (e.g., a field, a long hallway)

Vocabulary

- Supersonic
- Absorber
- Facets
- Radar signature
- Reconnaissance

Purpose

This challenge will improve students' understanding of:

- how radar works,
- characteristics related to reflecting radar,
- how radar is used in the military,
- how information is used for modifications and to make improvements,
- how to apply measurement skills with distance,
- how to convert standard measurements, and
- how to calculate averages.

Objectives

Students will demonstrate:

- an understanding of designing facets by creating a stealth aircraft,
- the ability to measure to the nearest eighth of an inch, and
- the ability to calculate averages.

Activity Preparation

1. Run off activity sheets.
2. Gather materials and place them in two different areas of the room.
3. Bookmark websites to be used in class.
   a. http://www.teachertube.com/viewVideo.php?video_id=214351&title=radar
   b. http://www.ausairpower.net/Profile-F-117A.html

Activity Procedure

1. Show video (2:51) on the development of radar at Link a.
2. Ask, "How has the development of radar impacted us?" and "How might radar possibly change the future?"
3. Show the picture of the F-117A Stealth Bomber, at Link b., to continue the discussion of being able to travel undetected.
4. Distribute the activity sheet to continue the discussion, and allow students to highlight information on the activity sheet.
5. Discuss the concept of reducing an object's radar signature.
6. Pass out pieces of 8.5" x 11" paper for students to continue working independently. Allow the students some time to do test flights with their stealth aircrafts.
7. While students are completing the independent activity, divide students into pairs to complete the team challenge.
8. Review the team challenge and answer any questions that students may have. Give the groups a few minutes to settle in before allowing one student from each pair to gather supplies. It's up to your discretion whether students can make their own designs of a stealth plane; however, the design must look like the stealth planes reviewed during the lesson.
9. Start the clock. After the allotted time has elapsed, announce that it is time for the competition.
10. After the competition, have students complete the activity sheets.
11. If you wish, assign one of the activities suggested in Extend the Learning With Stealth Aircraft: Activities.

Stealthy Design

GOAL

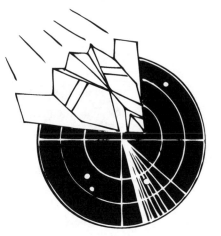

➤ Create a stealth aircraft that will travel the furthest distance.

MATERIALS

➤ 8.5" x 11" paper
➤ Metersticks or yardsticks

TIME TO CREATE

➤ 7 minutes

INDIVIDUAL ACTIVITY

Read the information below and highlight important information.

The idea of creating a stealth aircraft, an aircraft with the ability to travel undetected, was first conceived in the 1940s. The ability to fly without detection would not only improve military actions, it would also allow for reconnaissance (an exploratory military survey of enemy territory) to gain important information. All aircraft created a radar signature, a collection of elements that enabled radars to identify objects. The idea of a stealth aircraft was based on engineering an airplane with no radar signature, meaning that it could fly undetected by radars.

The first design was the U-2 spy plane, an aircraft able to fly at a very high altitude in order to reduce its radar signature. However, in 1954, the Soviets were able to easily detect the craft. The OXCART, developed in 1958, was able to fly at very high altitudes and travel at speeds beyond Mach 3, making it more elusive to radar. The OXCART was coated with special materials that absorbed radar energy, and parts were developed to "trap" radar energy and prevent it from traveling back to its source. Additionally, a chemical was added to the aircraft's fuel to reduce heat emissions. Even though the OXCART had a relatively small radar signature, it was still visible on radar.

After several modifications and failed attempts, the F-117, also known as the Stealth, was unveiled in 1989. The plane didn't look like a modern jet fighter. Instead of having a sleek, aerodynamic design, the F-117 was blocky and had many faceted surfaces (surfaces with flat parts). These surfaces created a reflection, causing a radar beam to be bounced in a different direction than the one from which it originated. The F-117 had a radar signature of about a hundredth of that of a conventional airplane, making the aircraft appear to be about the size of a bird on radarscopes.

Today's stealth bombers, the B-2 and the F-22, have a radar signature equivalent to that of a marble. Besides having specific surface geometry (to change the reflection), specific surface materials (to absorb radar), and modified exhaust (cooled to reduce heat signals), advancements in technology have allowed for engineers to design unmanned aircraft. Imagine what military abilities the armed forces will be able to produce in the future!

Hands-On Engineering © Prufrock Press Inc.   **59**

Permission is granted to photocopy or reproduce this page for single classroom use only.

1. What could be gained by having a small radar signature?

   _____

   _____

2. Build your own stealth airplane (without radar-absorbent coating):
   a. Fold a sheet of paper down the center like a hot dog, and open it out again.
   b. Take the first centimeter or 1/2" of the paper and fold it down.
   c. Fold the flap over and over until about 3/8 of the length of the sheet is folded.
   d. Fold the two top corners, bringing the top edges into the center line, and fold along the center line.
   e. Fold the wings down along the dotted line. Does it look like picture? If not, make modifications.

3. Do a test flight and record your results and observations. _____

   _____

   _____

4. What do you think the purpose of Step c. was? _____

   _____

   _____

TEAM CHALLENGE

The teacher will select groups of two for the team challenge and assign a number to each group. Once teams have been selected, the teacher will record the start time. You will have exactly 7 minutes to get your supplies and make your team's stealth airplane. Your goal is make a stealth aircraft that will travel the furthest distance.

Start Time _____ : _____ + 7 Minutes = _____ : _____ End Time

When the teacher signals that it is time to stop working, take the stealth aircrafts outside. Any team choosing to continue to work after teacher has signaled the stop time may be disqualified from the contest.

One member from each team lines up for the teacher to give the signal for the release of the aircraft. Another team member measures the distance from the start point. The members switch places for the second plane's opportunity. The goal is to have the plane with the farthest distance traveled from start to finish. Teams will have two flight opportunities per teammate. Distances must be recorded in the space provided.

1. Each team will take the best distance after four flight opportunities. Record the distances:

Teammate A's
Flight #1 _____ yd _____ ft _____ in.

Teammate A's
Flight #2 _____ yd _____ ft _____ in.

Teammate B's
Flight #1 _____ yd _____ ft _____ in.

Teammate B's
Flight #2 _____ yd _____ ft _____ in.

2. Compute the average distance travelled in inches of all four flights of your stealth aircraft.

Teammate A's plane average: _____ in.   Teammate B's plane average: _____ in.

Team's average: _____ in.

3. Compare the performance of the stealth aircraft you made with the performance of a traditional paper airplane.

Similarities: _____

_____

_____

Differences: _____

_____

_____

4. How might we use the concepts of radar technology in other areas of our lives, both today and in the future?

Today: _____

_____

_____

Future: _____

_____

_____

EXTEND THE LEARNING WITH STEALTH AIRCRAFT: ACTIVITIES

1. **History of stealth aircraft.** Toward the end of World War II, American troops discovered a facility in Germany with an advanced batwing-shaped jet fighter. Nazi engineers did not have time to complete their stealth fighter plane. If they'd had more time, how might this jet have changed the outcome of the war? Visit the following links, and then write a paragraph or two about how history may have been different and why:
   - Blueprint for Hitler's Horten 229 V3 stealth fighter: http://channel.nationalgeographic.com/channel/content/hitler-s-stealth-fighter-3942/albums/album-01.html
   - Video (3:25) about Hitler's stealth fighter: http://video.nationalgeographic.com/video/national-geographic-channel/specials-1/history-events/ngc-nazi-stealth-aircraft
   - Information on the history of military aviation: http://library.thinkquest.org/3142/aviation.htm

2. **Uses for radar in predicting the weather.** Extend your understanding of how radar comes into play in predicting the weather. Visit the following links, and then write a paragraph about the use of radar in weather prediction, focusing on radar's development and future in this field.
   - http://radar.weather.gov
   - http://www.intellicast.com/National/Radar/Forecast.aspx
   - http://www.weather.com/weather/map/interactive
   - http://www.hurricane.com/hurricane-radar-satellite.php
   - http://www.kirotv.com/interactive-radar/index.html

3. **Doppler radar.** A specialized radar called the Doppler radar beams a microwave signal toward a target and listens for its reflection. The frequency of the returned signal has been altered by the object's motion. Doppler radars are used in aviation, satellites, weather (meteorology), police speed radar guns, and radiology. Research Doppler radar and make a list of interesting facts you discover.

4. **The future of radar.** What applications might radar be used for in the future? Conduct online research, and use the business section of a daily newspaper to inform your discussion of radars and their potential applications. How might technology (e.g., smartphone apps) be aided by radars? How might apps change the uses of radars? Write a list of predictions regarding the future of radar uses and technology.

Whatever Floats Your Boat

Create a boat that can stay afloat for at least 1 minute while carrying the heaviest load.

Subjects and Skills

- Calculating the buoyancy and density of objects
- Relationship between buoyancy and density; displacement, weight, and density; Archimedes

Materials

- Clay
- Popsicle sticks
- One 2' x 2' sheet of foil per team
- Two corks per team
- One styrofoam plate per team
- Glue
- Golf balls, pennies, marbles, or other weight
- A sink or large container to hold water

Vocabulary

- Hull
- Density
- Buoyancy
- Archimedes
- Displacement

Purpose

This challenge will provide students with an understanding of:

- the relationship between buoyancy and density;
- the application of buoyancy in designing and engineering; and
- the basic concepts of displacement, weight, and density.

Objectives

Students will gain an understanding of:

- the relationships between buoyancy, density, displacement, and the weight of an object;
- Archimedes' principles of buoyancy;
- the development of hulls; and
- how math is applied to calculating the buoyancy and density of objects.

Activity Preparation

1. Run off activity sheets.
2. Gather materials and place them in two different areas of the room.
3. Bookmark websites to be used in class.
   a. http://www.gamequarium.org/cgi-bin/search/linfo.cgi?id=7898
   b. http://science.discovery.com/videos/what-the-ancients-knew-buoyancy-defined.html
   c. http://www.pbs.org/wgbh/nova/lasalle/buoybasics.html
   d. http://beityaacov2010.wikispaces.com/Archimedes

Activity Procedure

1. Ask questions to foster students' ideas about the buoyancy of objects (e.g., "Why do some objects sink while others float?" "How does a boat with an anchor inside it stay afloat, yet the anchor by itself would quickly sink?").
2. Write the word "displacement" on the board and ask about the definition and its possible relationship to the concept of buoyancy.
3. Watch Bill Nye's video (07:53) on buoyancy at Link a. and a video on displacement called *What the Ancients Knew: Buoyancy Defined* (01:06) at Link b.
4. Discuss the basic principles from the videos. Incorporate information from NOVA's Buoyancy Basics site at Link c.
5. Introduce Archimedes by visiting Archimedes of Syracuse: The Father of Buoyancy at Link d.
6. Distribute the activity sheets. As students work independently, prepare the materials by placing them in two different areas of the room, if you have not already done so. Divide students into teams to complete the team challenge, and assign each team a number.
7. Review the team challenge, and answer any questions students may have. After the competition is over, have students complete the activity sheets.
8. If you wish, assign one of the activities in Extend the Learning With Buoyancy: Activities.

Whatever Floats Your Boat

GOAL

➤ Make a boat that will stay afloat for at least 1 minute while carrying the most weight.

MATERIALS

➤ Clay
➤ Popsicle sticks
➤ One 2' x 2' sheet of foil per team
➤ One styrofoam plate per team
➤ Two corks per team
➤ Glue
➤ Golf balls, pennies, marbles, or other weight

TIME TO CREATE

➤ 20 minutes

INDIVIDUAL ACTIVITY

Read the information on hulls and buoyancy, and then answer the questions.

An object designed to float, such as a boat, is based on the scientific elements of buoyancy, displacement, and density. A man by the name of Archimedes was the first to articulate the aspects of buoyancy. His principle explains that an object's ability to float depends on the upward force, or displacement, of the water against the object. Think about this as a boat pushing down on the water as the water is pushing up. The water pushes up harder than the boat pushes down, so the boat is able to float. Archimedes' principle not only applies to buoyancy of ships and other vessels in water, but it also explains the rise of a balloon in the air and the apparent loss of weight of objects underwater.

The boat's hull—the body or frame of a boat—needs to be lighter than the amount of water that the boat is pushing away, or displacing. The very first hull is thought to have been created during the Stone Age, and was designed by hollowing out a tree trunk.

For an object to float, both weight and volume must be considered; the relative density, or weight per unit of volume, of the body compared to the fluid determines the buoyant force. The materials used to create a boat's hull must have a mass that, when divided by its volume, will provide a density of the boat equal to the amount of water displaced. When using steel, hulls are designed to trap air in order to lower the density ratio.

Hulls can be tapered, flat-bottomed, rounded, cathedral, or tunnel. Tapered hulls, like those seen in canoes, allow water to flow around the front, so that a boat can easily move through water. Draw a sketch of a tapered hull on the next page.

Hands-On Engineering © Prufrock Press Inc.

Permission is granted to photocopy or reproduce this page for single classroom use only.

65

SKETCH OF TAPERED HULL

Flat-bottomed hulls, commonly used to transport loads, are good for moving around in shallow water. They require careful balancing of cargo and passengers to prevent capsizing. Draw a sketch of a flat-bottomed hull.

SKETCH OF FLAT-BOTTOMED HULL

Rounded hulls glide through the water. They typically have a keel—a V-shaped extension of the hull along the centerline on the bottom—to prevent the boat from rolling too much. Draw a sketch of a rounded hull on the next page.

SKETCH OF ROUNDED HULL

```



```

1. Define density. _____

    _____

2. Define buoyancy. _____

    _____

3. Define displacement. _____

    _____

4. Draw the boat design you think will work best for today's challenge.

```



```

5. Why did you select that particular design? _____

_____

_____

6. What materials will be most helpful with the buoyancy of your boat?

_____

_____

Remember, if the boat's body is denser than the fluid it is in, it will sink. In calculating the buoyant force on a body, you must also consider the shape and position of the body. A steel rowboat placed on its front end into the water will sink, because the density of steel is much greater than that of water. However, in its normal position, the volume of the boat includes all of the air inside it, so its average density is then less than that of water, and it will float as a result.

TEAM CHALLENGE

Participants will work together in teams of two or three for a total of 20 minutes to design and build a boat using the materials provided that will float in a tub of water. The object is to build a boat that will hold as much weight as possible without sinking or spilling its contents. Your boat must stay afloat for at least 1 minute.

The teacher will select groups and assign group numbers. Once teams have been selected, the teacher will begin the time. You will have exactly 20 minutes to get your supplies and make your team's boat. If your team continues to work after the time is up, you may be disqualified.

Start Time _____ : _____ + 20 Minutes = _____ : _____ End Time

After the team challenge, answer the following questions.

1. How many golf balls was your boat able to hold? _____ How many marbles? _____ How many pennies? _____

2. What aspects of the various boat designs seemed to make them successful?

_____

_____

_____

3. What designs didn't seem to work well? _____

_____

_____

4. What is it about these designs that made them less successful? _____

   _____

   _____

   _____

   _____

5. How would you improve upon your boat design if you were able to rebuild for another challenge? _____

   _____

   _____

   _____

Hands-On Engineering © Prufrock Press Inc.

69

Permission is granted to photocopy or reproduce this page for single classroom use only.

EXTEND THE LEARNING WITH BUOYANCY: ACTIVITIES

1. **Advanced applications.** Visit http://www.pbs.org/wgbh/nova/teachers/ activities/3319_alicia.html to learn about negative, positive, and neutral buoyancy. Make a list of real-world applications for this information.
2. **Make your own submarine.** Follow the instructions below to make your own submarine. Once you've finished, write a paragraph explaining why this experiment works and what its real-world applications are.
   - Use a plastic bottle, a cap from a ballpoint pen, and modeling clay.
   - Make the submarine by putting clay on the end of pen cap (the part that points toward the nib).
   - Fill the bottle with water.
   - Put the submarine in the water.
   - Screw the bottle cap onto the bottle.
   - Squeeze the bottle and watch the submarine rise and fall.

Scrapers in the Sky

Build the tallest freestanding skyscraper that will hold the most weight.

Subjects and Skills

- Adaptation of materials and design elements
- The impact of nature on design
- The history of skyscrapers

Materials

- Newspaper
- Two pieces of 9"x 12" construction paper per team
- Tape
- Golf balls, pennies, or other weight

Vocabulary

- Skyscraper
- Industrial Revolution

Purpose

The principles behind skyscrapers link civil engineering concepts with science and history. When we study the fundamentals of skyscrapers, we are better able to understand the history of urban progress and development, and we can improve the way we plan cities in the future.

Objectives

Students will gain a better understanding of:
- the history of skyscrapers and the basic design principles behind their success;
- the forces that affect tall structures;
- the different structural engineering principles relating to skyscrapers; and
- the challenges faced by engineers in building tall structures.

Activity Preparation

1. Run off activity sheets.
2. Gather materials and place them in two different areas of the room.

3. Bookmark websites to be used in class.
    a. http://www.emporis.com/statistics/worlds-tallest-buildings
    b. http://www.pbs.org/wgbh/buildingbig/skyscraper/basics.html
    c. http://www.madehow.com/Volume-6/Skyscraper
    d. http://dsc.discovery.com/videos/we-built-this-city-new-york-skyscrapers.html
    e. http://science.discovery.com/videos/build-it-bigger-season-4-design-of-al-hamra.html

Activity Procedure

1. Introduce skyscrapers through images and information found at Link a.
2. Discuss the "Skyscraper Basics" from Link b.
3. Discuss how the advancement of materials and the invention of elevators changed the design of skyscrapers.
4. Discuss how design elements associated with skyscrapers can be seen in nature. Discuss what natural elements could influence or be incorporated into skyscraper design and construction.
5. For more detailed information on skyscrapers' history and design, go to Link c.
6. Distribute the activity sheets.
7. Show a video (03:00) on New York skyscrapers at Link d. to incorporate an understanding of the history and nature of the skyscrapers.
8. Discuss the design elements of the foundations of a skyscraper. Use a video of Al Hamra Tower (02:13) at Link e.
9. Review the team challenge with students and answer any questions they may have. For this challenge, students' structures are judged on two criteria: height and load-bearing capability. Each team's skyscraper will earn 1 point per inch of height from the base, and 1 point per unit of weight (e.g., golf ball, penny) to be placed on the top.
10. After the team challenge has concluded, have students finish their activity sheets.
11. If you wish, assign one of the activities suggested in Extend the Learning With Skyscrapers: Activities.

Scrapers in the Sky

GOAL

> Build the tallest freestanding skyscraper that will hold the most weight.

MATERIALS

> Newspaper
> Two pieces of 9"x 12" construction paper per team

> Tape
> Golf balls, pennies, or other weight

TIME TO CREATE

> 20 minutes

INDIVIDUAL ACTIVITY

Read the following and highlight the important information, and then answer the questions.

If you're walking in the center of a major city, you'll notice very tall buildings all around you. These buildings are known as skyscrapers. The first known grand construction was the Great Pyramid of Giza. Created around 450 B.C., the Great Pyramid of Giza was the tallest structure in the world for approximately 2,400 years, or until the 19th century during the Industrial Revolution. Fundamental changes in metal manufacturing occurred during the Industrial Revolution when two new lighter, yet sturdy, materials were developed: iron and steel.

Iron and steel allowed for new designs of very tall buildings. The 10-story Home Insurance Building in Chicago was the first "skyscraper" to be built using a steel frame. With lighter materials, even taller buildings could be designed, which brought to light a new problem: the wind. Engineers had to find ways to prevent the wind from causing the buildings to sway. Today's tallest skyscrapers are required to be 50 times stronger against wind elements than were the skyscrapers of the 1940s.

Strong foundations make it possible for skyscrapers to stand on the ground and are a significant element to the design. The location and the soil of a foundation must be large enough and strong enough to support a skyscraper. Therefore, the foundation is a signifi-cant component when considering the design. Geotechnical engineers are able to dig down to reach bedrock for better support; and in coastal areas, where the bedrock lies very deep under ground, concrete piles (long rods of concrete) are driven into the ground with a large diesel hammer until they hit the bedrock.

Several skyscrapers are famous for their height. The Willis Tower (formerly the Sears Tower), built in 1974, is 442 meters (1,450 ft) tall and has 110 floors. With 101 floors, Taiwan's

Hands-On Engineering © Prufrock Press Inc.

Permission is granted to photocopy or reproduce this page for single classroom use only.

73

Taipei 101 is 448 meters high and has an additional 508-meter spire (1,676 ft). In 2010, the Burj Khalifa, in Dubai, United Arab Emirates, standing at 828 meters (2,717 ft) with 160 floors, claimed the title of the tallest building in the world.

Extensive planning must take place when designing any building. In addition to considering the design and materials of a structure, engineers need to think about the center of gravity, weight distribution, base width, base support, surface area, and wind resistance.

1. What is the difference in height between the Burj Khalifa and the Willis Tower? _____

2. Besides the wind, what other concerns do engineers face when designing a building? _____

   _____

3. Towers used to be constructed of heavy stone. The rooms were dark and cramped, because windows would have weakened the structure. How have materials changed the design of tall structures? _____

   _____

4. How might engineers use the shape and function of natural forms in buildings? _____

   _____

TEAM CHALLENGE

Participants will work together in teams of two or three for a total of 20 minutes to design and build the tallest skyscraper possible with newspaper (can be cut, torn, or folded). The tallest skyscraper that will hold the most weight at the top will win. Each team's skyscraper will earn 1 point per inch of height from the base, and 1 point per unit of weight (e.g., golf ball, penny) to be placed on the top. The skyscraper must be mobile (so that it can be carried to the challenge site) and sturdy enough to hold weight at the top. Tape can only be used to attach paper to paper. Measure the height of the your skyscraper and test for sturdiness.

Once teams are selected, your teacher will begin the time. You will have 20 minutes to gather your materials and build your skyscraper. Once your teacher signals that time is up, you must stop working immediately and bring your skyscraper to the challenge site. Any team that continues to work after time has been called may be disqualified.

Start Time _____ : _____ + 20 Minutes = _____ : _____ End Time

After the team challenge, answer the following questions.
1. Why did you select the shape of your skyscraper? _____

   _____

2. Did you consider design elements visible in nature as you designed your skyscraper? How did this help you, or how could it have helped you? _____

   _____

3. How tall was your skyscraper, rounded to the nearest tenth of an inch? _____

4. How many units of weight was your skyscraper able to hold without toppling over? _____

5. What happened when your skyscraper was tested? _____

   _____

6. What would you do differently if you were to build another skyscraper? Why? _____

   _____

7. Consider the following concepts: center of gravity, weight distribution, base width, support of base, surface area, and wind resistance. What might be some basic rules of skyscraper design regarding two of these concepts? _____

   _____

8. How might skyscrapers change in the future?_____

   _____

9. How might skyscrapers be designed to protect against earthquakes?_____

   _____

EXTEND THE LEARNING WITH SKYSCRAPERS: ACTIVITIES

1. **Skyscraper challenge.** Take on the role of an engineer at Ace Forensic Engineering Lab by visiting http://www.pbs.org/wgbh/buildingbig/ skyscraper/challenge/index.html. Your job is to investigate skyscraper emergencies and then solve the problems that caused those emergencies.

2. **Forces affecting skyscrapers.** Learn about the different forces that affect skyscrapers by visiting http://www.pbs.org/wgbh/buildingbig/lab/loads. html. After the lesson, investigate forces in the site's interactive lab that simplifies the real-life forces that affect structures.

3. **Wind resistance.** Learn how engineers design skyscrapers to resist wind by visiting http://www.pbs.org/wgbh/buildingbig/skyscraper/ wind.html. Write a one-paragraph summary about wind resistance and skyscrapers.

4. **Interactive skyscraper maps.** Visit http://skyscraperpage.com/cities/ maps to learn more about specific skyscrapers using interactive maps. Buildings marked on a map can be clicked to open their information pages, and special controls allow you to customize what is shown on each map. Do you see patterns in where certain skyscrapers are built? Write a paragraph about what you learn at this site.

5. **Earthquake city simulation.** Build a city (with sugar cubes, bouillon cubes, and gelatin cubes) to put through simulated earthquakes to show the damage earthquakes can cause to buildings.
   1. Create a grid on large piece of cardboard by drawing four vertical lines and five horizontal lines. Each line should be 5 cm apart.
   2. Label the vertical lines 1st Avenue, 2nd Avenue, and so on, and label the horizontal lines A Street, B Street, and so on. This is the street grid of your city.
   3. Build three sugar-cube skyscrapers, each one five sugar cubes tall. Build the skyscrapers at the following corners: A and 1st , B and 2nd, and C and 3rd.
   4. Simulate an earthquake by tapping on the corner of D and 4th with the eraser of a pencil. Continue to tap until at least one cube from each skyscraper falls.

      Which skyscraper fell first? _____

      _____

      _____

In a real earthquake, would more damage happen in one place than another? Where would the most damage happen?

_____

_____

_____

5. Try the previous step again, reassembling the sugar cubes, but use different-strength taps to represent hard vibrations and soft vibrations. Determine how many hard or soft vibrations it takes to knock over buildings different distances away from the earthquake's epicenter.
6. Record your results in a chart containing the locations of the skyscrapers and when each fell.
7. Build a city of skyscrapers. Skyscrapers should include varying heights. Experiment with different types of cubes and designs. Try the pencil-tap test at a corner in the city to test the structures' ability to resist earthquakes.

Hands-On Engineering © Prufrock Press Inc.

77

Permission is granted to photocopy or reproduce this page for single classroom use only.

Parachute Express

Build a parachute that takes the longest time to descend.

Subjects and Skills

- Gravity, air resistance
- Surface area, weight, ratios
- The history of parachutes

Materials

- String or yarn
- Plastic garbage bags
- Adhesive dots or tape
- Paper clips
- A site from which to drop the parachutes (e.g., tall bookshelf, stairwell, window)

Vocabulary

- Gravity
- Air resistance
- Canopy
- Renaissance
- Parachute

Purpose

An understanding of how the principles of gravity and air resistance can be utilized is fundamental for gaining comprehension of physics topics.

Objectives

Students will gain a better understanding of:
- the history of the design of the parachute;
- the functions and uses of parachutes;
- how forces of gravity and air resistance can be used for productivity;
- how the design, surface area, shape, and weight of a parachute can impact its performance; and
- how Leonardo da Vinci's artistic abilities related to innovation and design.

Activity Preparation

1. Run off activity sheets.
2. Gather materials and place them in two different areas of the room.
3. Bookmark websites to be used in class.
   a. http://inventors.about.com/od/italianinventors/a/LeonardoDa Vinci.htm
   b. http://www.bbc.co.uk/schools/scienceclips/ages/10_11/forces_action_fs.shtml
   c. http://vimeo.com/38288667

Activity Procedure

1. Distribute the activity sheets and allow students to read and respond to Questions 1–3.
2. Ask students to share their responses.
3. Discuss Leonardo da Vinci's contributions by visiting Link a.
4. Have students continue to Question 4.
5. Brainstorm various ways in which parachutes have been used to help humankind. If there is time, continue the discussion to include possible uses for the future.
6. Discuss the terms *gravity*, *resistance*, *stability*, and *shape*. Ask how each of these can impact the performance of a parachute. To show how the weight of a parachute can change the speed of an object, go to Link b.
7. Introduce the term *canopy* (the part of the parachute that causes the air resistance). Ask students to discuss how the canopy's surface area impacts the parachute. (Canopies with a larger surface area produce more drag and therefore descend more slowly).
8. Before beginning the team challenge, review how to find the averages of data, as well as how to calculate surface area. If finding surface area is too advanced for your students, simply ask them to cross off Question 1 on the team challenge portion of their activity sheets.
9. Review the team challenge, and answer any questions that students may have. Ensure that all teams' parachutes are dropped from the same height.
10. Once the team challenge is completed, have students finish answering their questions.
11. Following the challenge, you may want to show the Extreme Parachuting (01:54) at Link c.
12. If you wish, assign one of the activities suggested in Extend the Learning With Parachutes: Activities.

Parachute Express

GOAL

> ➤ Build a parachute that takes the longest time to descend.

MATERIALS

> ➤ String or yarn
> ➤ Plastic garbage bags

> ➤ Paper clips
> ➤ Adhesive dots or tape

TIME TO CREATE

> ➤ 20 minutes

INDIVIDUAL ACTIVITY

Read the following, and then answer Questions 1–3. (Wait to continue until the teacher has instructed you to do so.)

Leonardo da Vinci was a remarkable Renaissance man who was very accomplished in many different disciplines—in fact, *Renaissance man* or *woman* has come to mean that somebody is known for significant accomplishments in multiple skill areas. Da Vinci was born in 1452 and is best known for his artwork, such as the Mona Lisa; however, in addition to showing artistic talent, da Vinci was a gifted scientist, with a strong curiosity and a creative vision of what was possible. Da Vinci conducted many experiments and created inventions well before modern science and invention as we know it had really begun. Many of his ideas for inventions and observations were meticulously sketched, with great attention to detail, in his journals. Highly curious, da Vinci created sketches that displayed a wide range of interests that often integrated art with math and science.

1. Think about air resistance. Which do you think would drop faster, a crumpled piece of paper, or one that was flat? Explain. _____

   _____

   _____

2. In your own words, define *parachute* and explain its purpose. _____

   _____

   _____

3. The first known written account of a parachute was found in da Vinci's notebooks from 1495; the first reported successful parachute jump wasn't made until 1783. How many years passed

before the concept of a parachute became a reality? _____. Why do you think it took so long? _____

_____

_____

4. Explain one way that parachutes are used today. _____

_____

_____

5. Some key concepts to understand when designing a parachute are gravity, air resistance, stability, and shape. How do gravity and air resistance impact a parachute?

_____

_____

How is shape related to stability of the parachute? _____

_____

_____

6. Leonardo's parachute sketches included proportional dimensions to allow a person to fall safely from a great height. Draw a sketch of a parachute. Include the measurements that would be appropriate to carry an adult.

7. Understanding basic physics concepts helps with the design of parachutes. Think about these concepts, and write down any ideas you may have about how modifying the parachute's design might impact its performance.

    a. changing the payload weight (the weight attached to the strings' base);
    b. lengthening, shortening, or changing the number of the suspension lines (strings attaching payload to parachute);
    c. increasing or decreasing the radius of the parachute, thus altering its size; and
    d. cutting holes and/or slits in the parachute fabric.

    _____

    _____

TEAM CHALLENGE

Participants will work together in teams of two or three for a total of 20 minutes to build a parachute with the most air resistance. The goal is to create a parachute that has the slowest descent (travel time from the release to the landing). Using the materials provided, build a parachute that, when weight is attached, will have the slowest descent. (All teams' parachutes will be dropped from the same height.)

The teacher will select groups and assign group numbers. Once the teacher starts the time, your group will have 20 minutes to gather supplies and design your parachute. Once the teacher signals that time is up, stop working immediately and bring your parachute to the test site. Any team that continues to work after time has been called may be disqualified.

> Start Time _____ : _____ + 20 Minutes = _____ : _____ End Time

1. What is the surface area of your parachute's canopy? _____

2. Record the time of each team's parachute:

Parachute Times

Team 1 _____ : _____	Team 5 _____ : _____	Team 9 _____ : _____
Team 2 _____ : _____	Team 6 _____ : _____	Team 10 _____ : _____
Team 3 _____ : _____	Team 7 _____ : _____	Team 11 _____ : _____
Team 4 _____ : _____	Team 8 _____ : _____	Team 12 _____ : _____

3. What was the average time that it took for a team's parachute to descend?

    Average time for descent: _____ : _____

4. How did your parachute's time compare with the class average? _____

    _____

    _____

5. What is a contributing factor for a parachute to stay in the air longer, and why?

_____

_____

6. How would you modify your parachute to improve your design?_____

_____

_____

7. Parachutes have many uses. One way meteorologists use parachutes is for measuring the atmosphere over the oceans. Dropwindsondes, instruments used to measure pressure, temperature, humidity, and wind, are attached to parachutes and then dropped from an airplane. As they float down toward the ocean, they radio atmospheric information back to the airplane. Think about some of the concerns we have on Earth. How might we use parachutes to address those concerns?_____

_____

_____

Hands-On Engineering © Prufrock Press Inc.

Permission is granted to photocopy or reproduce this page for single classroom use only.

83

EXTEND THE LEARNING WITH PARACHUTES: ACTIVITIES

1. **Design a parachute.** Visit NOVA's Mars exploration rover mission site and complete the interactive lesson at http://www.pbs.org/wgbh/nova/space/design-mars-parachute.html. You will design a parachute to help the Mars exploration rovers *Spirit* and *Opportunity* touch down safely on the red planet.

2. **Surface area.** At what point does increasing the size of a parachute no longer increase its effectiveness? Make several different parachutes with various canopy sizes. Test them, and record your results in a chart. Write a brief report about your findings.

3. **Literature connection:** Read Michael O. Tunnell's *Candy Bomber: The Story of the Berlin Airlift's "Chocolate Pilot."* Draw a picture depicting a scene from the book that features parachutes.

4. **Everyday materials.** Build a better parachute with materials you find around your house. Bring the parachute to school.

It's So Simple Machines

The purpose of this activity is to learn about simple machines. There is no team challenge associated with this lesson; however, the understanding of simple machines will be important for students to know for future challenges.

Subjects and Skills
- The use of machines to make work easier
- Geometry

Materials Needed
- Rulers
- Pencil sharpeners
- Wedges
- Other examples of simple machines

Vocabulary
- Work
- Force
- Effort
- Simple machines
- Complex machines
- Lever
- Pulley
- Inclined plane
- Wedge
- Screw
- Wheel and axle

Purpose
An understanding of simple machines is fundamental for developing an understanding of physics concepts.

Objectives
Students will gain a better understanding of:
- the difference between simple and complex machines;
- the six types of simple machines;

It's So Simple Machines

- how simple machines make work easier, but do not reduce the amount of work;
- calculating work using Newtons and Joules; and
- the simple machines around us.

Activity Preparation

1. Run off activity sheets and the Instructor Key. The students should complete the chart over the course of several days.
2. Gather materials: rulers, pencil sharpeners, wedges, and other items to use as examples of simple machines.
3. Bookmark websites to be used in class.
   a. https://vimeo.com/38290259
   b. http://www.mikids.com/Smachines.htm
   c. http://www.angelfire.com/ego/mr.f/SubjectLinks/science/movies gr8/1work.swf
   d. https://vimeo.com/38291275
   e. https://vimeo.com/38290616
   f. http://atlantis.coe.uh.edu/archive/science/science_lessons/scienceles1/finalhome.htm

Activity Procedure

1. Explain that there are six types of simple machines. Show examples of each type of simple machine. Explain the definition of a machine (a machine is any device that makes work easier), as well as the definition of a simple machine (a machine with one working part).
2. Distribute the activity sheets to continue the class discussion, using the activity sheet as a guide. It is up to you how much time to devote to this lesson. If time is available, this lesson would be best taught within two class periods, with a 2- or 3-day break in between to allow students extra time to complete their charts.
3. Show the video (05:45) on simple machines at Link a.
4. For Question 1 on the activity sheet, use the simple machine images at Link b. Continue through Question 5. When the students have finished, discuss the answers for Questions 1–5. (For Questions 4 and 5, *force* is the pull or the push on an object, resulting in its movement, and *distance* is the space that the object moves.)
5. Introduce the terms *Newton* and *Joule* by watching BrainPOP video (02:20) at Link c.
6. Continue to Question 6 on the activity sheet. Here are explanations of the answers:
   a. Work = Force x Distance, so $(100)(50)(0) = 0$.

   b. The boy applies force that moves the cat 2 m. Work = (90)(10)(2) = 1,800 Newton meters or Joules.

7. Show the video (05:23) on ramps at Link d.

8. Discuss friction. Friction is a force that slows down or stops motion. It's caused when two parts rub against each other. Friction can be reduced by using grease or oil or by adding wheels.

9. Show the video (06:05) on pulleys at Link e.

10. Distribute the worksheet on simple machines. Have students complete the chart according to the timeline that is most convenient for your class, and give them whatever resources you choose (e.g., library, Internet).

11. Review the chart, and then follow up with the information included on the attached Instructor Key.

12. Have students take the quiz at Link f.

It's So Simple Machines

There is no team challenge associated with this lesson. However, you will be able to use the information you learn in this lesson to complete future challenges.

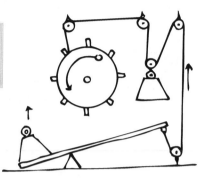

Read the following information and answer the questions while you discuss simple machines as a class.

A machine is any device that makes work easier. There are simple and complex machines. Simple machines are called "simple" because most have only one moving part. When you put simple machines together, you get a complex machine.

1. Draw and label each of the six simple machines.

_____ _____ _____

_____ _____ _____

2. Define *machine*. _____

_____

_____

3. What is a simple machine? _____

_____

_____

All simple machines require human energy in order to function. Even though using simple machines makes the work easier, the same amount of work is actually being accomplished. The difference is that a simple machine reduces the amount of effort required to do the work or accomplish the job. When we use a simple machine to move something, we actually need to go a greater distance to accomplish the same amount of work. The energy has been modified, or traded. The muscle work has been traded for legwork, or preparation.

Think about a location that has both stairs and a ramp for people to go from a lower area to a higher area. A ramp reduces the amount of effort and strength (force) required to move up in the room; however, the actual distance traveled is increased. The amount of actual work done is the same.

Make a drawing of the example above (stairs vs. ramp), providing a written explanation of the relationship between effort, distance, and work on the drawing.

Scientifically speaking, work only occurs when something is moved. If you are pushing on a wall, you may get tired, but you are not actually doing work. If you didn't move the wall, then scientifically, you didn't do any work.

Hands-On Engineering © Prufrock Press Inc.

89

Permission is granted to photocopy or reproduce this page for single classroom use only.

There are two components to work: force and distance. The amount of force is the pushing and/or pulling required to do the work. Distance is the how far the load (what has moved) has traveled once force has been applied. This formula is helpful: Work = Force x Distance. The work done is the force exerted multiplied by the distance moved.

4. Force is: _____

_____

5. Distance is: _____

_____

Work is measured in Joules (after James Prescott Joule). Force is measured in Newtons (after Sir Isaac Newton). Distance is measured in meters, m.

6. Try solving these two problems. Use the information you just learned.

    a. A 100-pound girl sits on a 50-pound bench. How much work is done on the bench?

    _____

    b. A 90-pound boy lifts a 10-pound cat 2 meters to the right. How much work did he do?

    _____

7. Rub your hands together. You've just created friction. What is friction? _____

_____

_____

8. How can you reduce friction? _____

_____

_____

9. Complete the Simple Machines worksheet.

Name: _____ Date: _____

Simple Machines

Simple Machine	Definition and Description	Function	Examples
LEVER			
INCLINED PLANE			
SCREW			
WHEEL AND AXLE			
PULLEY			
WEDGE			

Instructor Key

Simple Machine	Definition and Description	Function	Examples
LEVER	A lever is a board that rests on a support called a fulcrum. The balance point, or fulcrum, is between the applied force and the load. A simple lever has three parts: the fulcrum (balance point), the effort arm (where force or work is applied), and the resistance arm (where the object to be moved is placed).	Lifts or moves loads	Nutcracker, seesaw, crowbar, elbow, tweezers, bottle opener
INCLINED PLANE	An inclined plane is a slanting surface connecting a lower level to a higher level. The ramp is an inclined plane. Although the distance up the ramp is greater than the distance straight up, less force is required to move the load over this greater distance.	Moves loads up or down a ramp	Slide, stairs, ramp, escalator, slope
SCREW	The screw is actually just another kind of inclined plane. It is basically an inclined plane that is wrapped around a cylinder.	Fastens or tightens one object to another	Cork screw, swivel chair, door lock
WHEEL AND AXLE	A rod called an axle can be put through a wheel so that they both move together.	Lifts or moves loads	Wagon, pencil sharpener, bike, electric fan

Hands-On Engineering © Prufrock Press Inc.

Instructor Key, continued

Simple Machine	Definition and Description	Function	Examples
PULLEY	A rope or cable is put through a grooved wheel that turns, moving the rope or cable through and around it.	Moves things up, down, or across	Curtain rod, mini-blind, fishing rod, flag pole, crane
WEDGE	An object with at least one slanted side ending in a sharp edge.	Pushes two objects apart	Knives, forks, nails

Catapult to the Front of the Line

Create a catapult that will hurl a penny through a target from the furthest distance away.

Subjects and Skills

- The effect of changing fulcrum placement
- Effort, resistance, work
- The history of catapults

Materials

- Popsicle sticks
- Clothespins
- Rubber bands
- String or yarn
- One plastic spoon per team
- Pennies (for catapulting)
- A hula hoop (or other target through which pennies can be flung)

Vocabulary

- Mangonel
- Ballista
- Trebuchet
- Torsion
- Lever
- Fulcrum
- Load
- Effort

Purpose

Understanding the principles of levers is important for developing an understanding of Class 2 simple machines. Students will learn how a lever's fulcrum point can impact the effort necessary to lift the load.

Objectives

Students will gain a better understanding of:
- the history of the basic design of the catapult,
- how the lever system can be changed by moving the position of the load and fulcrum,

- how effort is the force needed to move a load or overcome a resistance, and
- how a catapult's design can impact its performance.

Activity Preparation

1. Run off activity sheets.
2. Gather materials and place them in two different areas of the room.
3. Bookmark websites to be used in class.
   a. http://www.catapults.info
   b. http://www.schoolhistory.co.uk/games/fling
   c. http://en.wikibooks.org/wiki/Wikijunior:How_Things_Work/Lever
   d. http://www1.teachertube.com/viewVideo.php?video_id=2387 58&title=Trebuchets__amp__Catapults
   e. http://www.teachertube.com/viewVideo.php?video_id=238841& title=Roman_Catapult&vpkey=

Activity Procedure

1. Distribute the activity sheets. Read and discuss the information.
2. Go to Link a. for pictures of each type of catapult to layer students' understanding. Continue the discussion.
3. Ask, "What do you think may have been a problem with using the mangonel in a battle?" Guide students to understand that the weight of the mangonel, as well as its slowness to move and its difficulty to load, were problematic.
4. Have students use their own arms to demonstrate the flinging motion. (Students may need to be warned to maintain their personal space.)
5. For active engagement in demonstrating the flinging action, visit Fling the Teacher at Link b. Select a topic, or create your own topic, for your students to play.
6. Teach how levers work using information available at Link c.
7. Show the Trebuchets & Catapults video (04:19) at Link d.
8. Discuss the fulcrum. The fulcrum is the point where a lever is free to rotate. In a seesaw, the fulcrum is the middle support that the lever rests on.
9. Have students draw and label the lever, fulcrum, and load.
10. Before students continue to the team challenge, show the video (02:53) What the Ancients Knew: The Roman Catapult at Link e.
11. Put students in groups of two or three and assign group numbers.
12. Review the team challenge, answering any questions that students may have. Conduct the challenge in whatever manner is most convenient and appropriate for your classroom. If students' catapults are able to hurl the

penny through the target, they can move their catapults further and further away to see what the greatest distances are from which their catapults will be effective. You may, however, want to institute a cap on how many trials each team is allowed.

13. After the challenge has been completed, have students finish their activity sheets.

14. If you wish, assign one of the activities suggested in Extend the Learning With Catapults: Activities.

Catapult to the Front of the Line

GOAL

> ➤ Create a catapult that will hurl a penny through a target from the furthest distance away.

MATERIALS

> ➤ Popsicle sticks
> ➤ Clothespins
> ➤ Rubber bands
> ➤ String or yarn
> ➤ One plastic spoon per team
> ➤ Pennies (for catapulting)

TIME TO CREATE

> ➤ 25 minutes

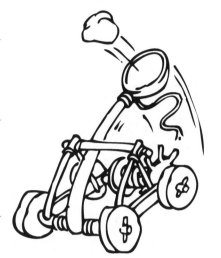

INDIVIDUAL ACTIVITY

Read the following, highlighting important information, and answer the questions.

Imagine that you are in the midst of a snowball fight. In addition to preparing for battle, you also need to think about protection. Hiding behind something is helpful, but what if your enemy is able to break down your barrier? Throughout history, finding a way to destroy the enemy's protection while maintaining a safe distance was challenging—until the invention of the catapult, the one-armed throwing machine.

Ancient Greeks referred to the catapult as a mangonel, meaning "engine of war." The mangonel, weighing approximately 2 tons, functioned by flinging heavy objects over and through walls. Because of its powerful kicking motion, mangonels were also referred to as onagers, a name derived from onagros, meaning "wild donkey."

A ballista was another type of catapult. It was designed similarly to the crossbow. Ballistas relied on the work of torsion to release ammunition that looked like giant arrows.

Over time, gravity catapults, such as the trebuchet, were invented. Trebuchets were designed to hurl a heavy object into a high arc, which was quite useful for breaking down castle walls, especially if the ammunition involved fire. Catapults have been one of the most effective weapons for warfare.

A sling is attached to the end of the catapult's arm. In lowering the arm, the user stores energy in the ropes, and when the arm is released, the arm is flung forward. The force contained in the ropes is at its greatest when the arm first starts to move, and at its least when it hits a padded buffer, which acts as a stopper. This rapid stop allows the object to leave the sling at maximum speed before stopping. Adjusting the length of the ropes allows for the thrown object to aim more accurately at the target.

A lever can help to move or lift objects by applying force to gain a mechanical advantage. The lever has two important parts: a fulcrum, or center of rotation, and a force arm, which is the lever itself. To use the lever, four parts work together: the lever (which is long and rigid), the fulcrum (the resting point on which the lever turns or pivots), the effort (the force that is applied), and the load (the object that will be moved).

1. What do you think may have been problematic about using the mangonel in a battle?

_____

_____

2. Draw and label the lever, fulcrum, and load.

TEAM CHALLENGE

Participants will work together in teams of two or three for a total of 25 minutes to make a mangonel that can toss a penny through a target. The mangonel must be on the floor and must have a trigger mechanism (it cannot be a person) to launch the penny. A team can win by making a mangonel that is able to hurl the penny through the target from the furthest distance away. Once the teacher starts the time, your team will have 25 minutes to gather your supplies and build your mangonel. After the teacher signals that time is up, you must stop working immediately and take your catapult to the designated challenge site. Any team that continues to work after time has been called may be disqualified.

Start Time _____ : _____ + 25 Minutes = _____ : _____ End Time

Keep these concepts in mind when making your mangonel:
➤ the weight of the object thrown,
➤ the strength and length of the arm,
➤ the flexibility and speed of the arm, and
➤ the angle and height of the launch.

During the team challenge, record the results.

CATAPULTS' DISTANCES FROM TARGET

Team 1: _____ft _____in.   Team 2: _____ft _____in.   Team 3: _____ft _____in.

Team 4: _____ft _____in.   Team 5: _____ft _____in.   Team 6: _____ft _____in.

Team 7: _____ft _____in.   Team 8: _____ft _____in.   Team 9: _____ft _____in.

Team 10: _____ft _____in.   Team 11: _____ft _____in.   Team 12: _____ft _____in.

Team 13: _____ft _____in.   Team 14: _____ft _____in.   Team 15: _____ft _____in.

After the team challenge, complete the following questions.

1. What did you use for the lever? _____

2. What did you use to create tension? _____

3. What was the difference between your object's distance from the target and the object closest to the target? _____ft _____in.

4. What contributed to the success of the winning mangonel? _____

    _____

    _____

5. What would you do differently to refine your mangonel? _____

    _____

    _____

EXTEND THE LEARNING WITH CATAPULTS: ACTIVITIES

1. **Velocity ratio and pulleys.** Visit http://www.technologystudent.com/gears1/pulley2.htm to learn and apply different methods of using what we've discussed in class. Print and complete the practice sheet.

2. **Interactive catapult.** Visit http://kids.discovery.com/games/just-for-fun/catapult to see an online replica of an ancient catapult. Discuss how this model is similar to and different from the catapult your team made in a complete paragraph.

3. **Fling the teacher.** Using the template available at http://www.schoolhistory.co.uk/games/fling/, select an academic topic that relates to something you've been studying in another subject. Record the 15 questions and answers that you respond to correctly to fling the teacher.

4. **Simple machines.** Visit http://www.technologystudent.com/forcmom/lever1.htm and http://www.enchantedlearning.com/physics/machines/Levers.shtml. Compare and contrast the different levers: Class 1, Class 2, and Class 3. Create a chart to show the lever, load, fulcrum, mechanical advantages, equal-arm balance, and effort of each type. Include drawings.

Be a Cooper

Build a barrel to hold and safely transport the most weight for a distance of 20 feet. (More weight will be added until only one barrel remains.)

Subjects and Skills

- Area, circumference, volume, nets
- The history of casks

Materials

- Straws
- Index cards
- Construction paper
- Paper cups
- Weight (e.g., marbles, pennies, golf balls)

Vocabulary

- Cooper
- Versatile
- Staves
- Gauging
- Net
- Diameter
- Circumference
- Volume

Purpose

Students will learn and apply geometric skills by connecting concepts with history. Understanding how to find the volume of a cask requires multiple mathematical skills necessary for students to understand broader geometric concepts.

Objectives

Students will gain a better understanding of:
- the history of the design of the cask,
- drawing a net of a solid,
- finding the area of a circle,
- finding the circumference of a circle, and
- finding the volume of a cylindrical solid.

Activity Preparation

1. Run off activity sheets.
2. Gather materials and place in two different areas of the classroom.
3. Bookmark websites to be used in class.
   a. http://www.history.org/Foundation/journal/Autumn03/cooper slideshow
   b. http://www.scholastic.com/teachers/article/mayflower-john -alden-ships-cooper
   c. http://www.rootsweb.ancestry.com/~flbbm/heritage/cooper/ barrelmaking.htm
   d. http://www.history.org/kids/games/cooperation.cfm
   e. http://www.britishpathe.com/record.php?id=46792
   f. http://vimeo.com/5391598

Activity Procedure

1. Introduce the term *cooper*. Explain that a cooper is someone who makes casks, or barrels. Show the slideshow from Colonial Williamsburg at Link a.
2. Review the mock interview with John Alden, hired to be the cooper on the *Mayflower* in 1621, at Link b.
3. Distribute the activity sheets. Have students read along and define versatile (adaptable).
4. Continue reading together. For images and information about barrel parts, use the information at Link c. An excellent interactive activity is available through Colonial Williamsburg at Link d.
5. Have students draw the net on their activity sheets.
6. Check for understanding of geometric concepts. Review how to find the volume of cylinders, if necessary.
7. Show the video about barrel making (03:19) at Link e. or the video (02:51) at Link f.
8. Review the correct answers for the activity sheet. For Question 4, the diameter is 6 inches, the radius is 3 inches, the circumference is 18.84 inches, the area is 28.26 square inches, and the volume is 141.3 cubic inches.
9. Review the team challenge.
10. Once the challenge has been completed, have students finish filling out their sheets.
11. If you wish, assign one of the activities in Extend the Learning With Casks: Activities.

Be a Cooper

GOAL

➢ Build a barrel to hold and safely transport the most weight for a distance of 20 feet. (More weight will be added until only one barrel remains.)

MATERIALS

➢ Straws
➢ Construction paper
➢ Index cards
➢ Paper cups
➢ Weight (e.g., marbles, pennies, golf balls)

TIME TO CREATE

➢ 20 minutes

INDIVIDUAL ACTIVITY

Read the following, highlighting important information, and then answer the questions.

Coopers were craftsmen who made casks, which are similar to barrels. At one time, the durable casks were essential for storing everything from gunpowder to milk. Casks were tough and versatile, and because of their round shape, they were easily moved. Traders in the 1700s depended on casks for shipping their wares, such as flour, wine, shoes, books, and leeches (used in medicine) to other countries. By the 1750s, British coopers made hundreds of thousands of casks annually.

Casks have a flat bottom and a flat lid. Their sides are shaped from wooden staves (narrow strips of wood) held together by iron bands. The staves are slightly wider in the middle, which causes the barrel to be rounded and not cylindrical in shape.

Because many products were transported and sold in barrels years ago, computing the volume of a barrel was an important skill. It was called gauging (estimating an amount). Calculating with accuracy was difficult because of the barrel's shape; therefore, gauging the volume of a barrel was to calculate its area as if it were a cylinder.

1. Define *versatile*: _____

_____

2. A *net* is a two-dimensional shape that can be folded into a geometric solid. Draw a net of a cask.

3. What is the formula to calculate the circumference of a circle? _____

What is the formula to calculate the area of a circle? _____

What is the formula to calculate the volume of a cylinder? _____

4. What is the length of the diameter in the cylinder below? _____

What is the radius? _____

What is the circumference of the top? _____

What is the area of the bottom? _____

What is the volume? _____

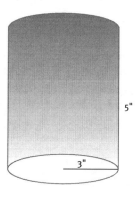

5"

3"

TEAM CHALLENGE

Participants will work together in teams of two or three for a total of 20 minutes to make a cask from the materials provided. The cask needs to safely transport the heaviest load from one location to another, roughly the length of your classroom. Once the teacher starts the time, you will have exactly 20 minutes to gather your materials and build your cask. Once the teacher signals that time is up, you must stop working immediately and take your cask to the designated challenge site. Any team that continues to work after time has been called may be disqualified.

1. What is the length of the diameter in your cylinder? _____

    What is the length of the radius? _____

    What is the circumference of the top? _____

    What is the area of the bottom? _____

    What is the volume of your cask? _____

2. What was the distance your cask was able to transport weight safely? _____ft _____ in.
3. What was the heaviest load your cask was able to carry? _____
4. Were there any problems in your team's cask's design? Explain your answer.

    _____

    _____

5. How far was the most successful cask able to travel? _____ft _____ in.
6. Explain what contributed to the cask's success in transporting weight the furthest.

    _____

    _____

7. What was the difference between your cask's distance traveled and the distance traveled by the most successful cask? _____ft _____ in.
8. Explain the most important contributing element to the design of a cask for sturdiness.

    _____

    _____

9. What specific materials might be used for a cask that needed to transport liquid or be transported in water? _____

    _____

    _____

10. How would you improve on the design and/or crafting of your cask? _____

    _____

    _____

Hands-On Engineering © Prufrock Press Inc.

Permission is granted to photocopy or reproduce this page for single classroom use only.

105

EXTEND THE LEARNING WITH CASKS: ACTIVITIES

1. **Learn about Kepler.** Johannes Kepler (1571–1630) was the first to figure out that the paths planets make around the sun are ellipses; this is Kepler's first law of planetary motion. Kepler also came up with other laws, one of which is the formula for finding the volume of a barrel. Research Kepler and write a page-long summary of what you've learned about him, focusing on his work with barrels.

2. **Volume of a barrel.** Using what you know about finding the volume of a cylinder, consider what important elements would need to be considered if you were to find the volume of a barrel. Draw a cylinder and a barrel on a separate sheet of paper. Add a radius both in the top and in the middle of each solid. Write a paragraph explaining the differences between the two solids regarding volume, and speculate about how the middle radius might be used to find the formula for the volume of a cylinder. Once you've written this paragraph, conduct research to find the formula for finding the area of a barrel. Write a second paragraph explaining how this formula relates to your expectations and predictions.

3. **Rain barrels.** Visit http://www.naturalrainwater.com/make_rain barrel.htm; http://www.cityofbremerton.com/content/sw_makeyourown rainbarrel.html; and http://www.youtube.com/watch?v=q8_72a9BDH U&feature=related to research making a rain barrel (used to collect the rain that runs off of your roof during a rainstorm). Construct a rain barrel and measure how much water it collects the next time it rains. Take a photo of your rain barrel, and bring it in with a results sheet.

Hands-On Engineering © Prufrock Press Inc.

Whirlybird Liftoff

Build a helicopter that will hover in the air for the longest duration.

Subjects and Skills

- Air mass, air resistance, lift
- Calculating scale
- Physics concepts

Materials

- Large index cards
- 8.5" x 11" paper
- Construction paper
- Rulers
- Paper clips

Vocabulary

- Lift
- Rotorcraft
- Airfoil

Purpose

Students will apply math skills as they learn how air resistance creates lift.

Objectives

Students will gain a better understanding of:
- the history of helicopter design,
- how lift occurs,
- air mass,
- changing the scale with division, and
- timing a helicopter's descent.

Activity Preparation

1. Run off activity sheets.
2. Gather materials and place them in two different areas of the room.
3. Bookmark websites to be used in class.
   a. http://www.history.com/shows/ancient-discoveries/videos/ancient-hobbyist-taketombo#ancient-hobbyist-taketombo

    b. http://www.mos.org/sln/Leonardo/Leo-Copter.html

    c. http://www.sikorskyarchives.com

    d. http://videos.howstuffworks.com/nasa/2139-how-helicopters-work-video.htm

    e. http://videos.howstuffworks.com/discovery/7075-greatest-ever-the-most-powerful-helicopter-video.htm

Activity Procedure

1. Show a video of China's bamboo dragonfly (02:07) at Link a.
2. Ask students what modern-day creation this toy reminds them of.
3. Show the image of Leonardo da Vinci's sketch from 1480 at Link b. and ask students what they think it represents. Explain that today's challenge is going to tie in concepts from ancient China and Leonardo da Vinci's sketches.
4. Distribute the activity sheets for students to read, highlight, and discuss. Use images from Link c. in the discussion of Igor Sikorsky's design.
5. Visit Link d. to show a video (04:45) about how helicopters fly to explain how rotors create force.
6. Distribute paper for students to use to make helicopters and experiment with rotors to create lift.
7. While students are making helicopters, put students into small groups and assign group numbers.
8. Discuss what students learned from their individual experimentation with paper (e.g., changing size and/or shape of wings affects speed, air pushes up against wings, more contact between blades and air results in slower descent).
9. Review the team challenge, and answer any questions students may have. Hold the challenge in whatever manner is most convenient and appropriate for your classroom.
10. Once the challenge has been completed, have students finish answering the questions on their sheets.
11. Review the teams' responses to Questions 1–9 on the activity sheet.
12. Show the video (03.38) at Link e. about the most powerful helicopter and discuss its design.
13. If you wish, assign one of the activities suggested in Extend the Learning With Helicopters: Activities.

Whirlybird Liftoff

GOAL

➢ Build a helicopter that will hover in the air for the longest duration.

MATERIALS

➢ Large index cards
➢ 8.5" x 11" paper
➢ Paper clips
➢ Construction paper
➢ Rulers

TIME TO CREATE

➢ 20 minutes

INDIVIDUAL ACTIVITY

Read the following, highlight important information, and respond to the prompts.

Helicopter flight goes back to around 400 B.C. and can be attributed to an ancient Chinese toy: the bamboo dragon. The toy consists of a piece of wood with a blade attached to the top with a dowel. Children would spin the stick between their hands, generating lift, and then release it into the air to take flight.

Draw a sketch of what the bamboo dragon might have looked like.

Leonardo da Vinci's (1493) notebooks included sketches of an ornithopter flying machine. His design included a rotating screw that was to be powered by a wind-up spring.

Nearly 500 years later, incorporating da Vinci's designs, Igor Sikorsky set out to build the first helicopter capable of carrying a person on a vertical flight. After many attempts spanning from 1910–1940, Sikorsky was able to achieve success with a helicopter design that used a main lifting rotor and a tail rotor to create a lift. The Sikorsky VS-300 was the first working helicopter and served as the forerunner for the helicopters used today.

Pioneers of vertical flight needed a true understanding of the nature of lift caused by an efficient propeller design. A propeller is an airfoil: a curved surface that can generate lift when air moves over it. When air moves over the surface of a rotating propeller, the air pressure on top is reduced, and the air pressure underneath is increased. The combined pressures generate the lift needed to push the helicopter up.

When designing an efficient propeller, engineers need to think about two principles: the radius of the propeller (the distance from the center to the tip), and the twist angle of the propeller (the angle of the propeller blade). The radius and twist angle of the propellers should remain constant, while the chord lengths of each should vary. (Understanding the chord length, the straight-line width of the propeller at a given distance along the radius, is also important, but for now, we're going to set that idea aside.)

Make your own helicopter by using paper or index cards.
➢ Draw the design as seen in the figure. Cut along dotted lines.
➢ Fold the flaps forward and backward as shown.
➢ Fold flaps forward along the dotted lines as shown.
➢ Fold along the line upward as shown and attach a paper clip to the flap.
➢ Your helicopter should look like the figure shown. The blades should spin rapidly, creating lift and allowing the helicopter to fall to the ground slowly.

Now make other helicopters, using the materials provided, with different variations to see how the changes you make affect the speed of the blades' spin and how quickly the helicopter falls to the ground. What happens if you shorten the helicopter blades? _____

TEAM CHALLENGE

Participants will work together in teams of two or three for a total of 20 minutes to make two helicopters per team. One helicopter will be half of the scale as the one made during the individual activity. The other will be made with construction paper and will be approximately 33% larger than the size of the one made during the individual activity. The goal is to make a helicopter that will stay in the air the longest time.

Once the teacher starts the time, your team will have exactly 20 minutes to gather your activities and build your helicopters. Once your teacher signals that time is up, stop working immediately and proceed with your helicopters to the challenge site. Any team that continues to work after the time is up may be disqualified.

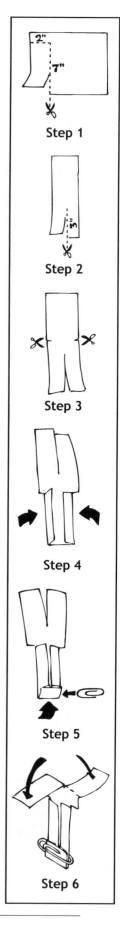

Step 1

Step 2

Step 3

Step 4

Step 5

Step 6

Start Time _____ : _____ + 20 Minutes = _____ : _____ End Time

Run two tests for each helicopter. Circle the best time for each helicopter. That will be the time counted toward the challenge.

1. Record your helicopters' best times:

   Small helicopter: _____

   Medium helicopter: _____

   Big helicopter: _____

2. What are the dimensions of the smallest helicopter? _____

3. What are the dimensions of the largest helicopter? _____

4. Which direction does the helicopter spin as it falls, clockwise or counterclockwise? _____

5. What happens if you bend the blades of the helicopter in the opposite directions? _____

6. Which of the three helicopters has the best hovering ability? _____

7. Which of the three helicopters has the best accuracy or handling ability? _____

8. Compare the results of your team's helicopters with another team's helicopter times. Discuss what made one size better than another. Write down the other team's helicopters' times here:

   Small helicopter: _____ : _____

   Medium helicopter: _____ : _____

   Big helicopter: _____ : _____

9. Explain similarities and/or differences that you found among your team's helicopters and the other team's helicopters: _____

   _____

   _____

10. If you were to make another helicopter, what size and materials would you use? Explain your response. _____

   _____

   _____

Hands-On Engineering © Prufrock Press Inc.

Permission is granted to photocopy or reproduce this page for single classroom use only.

111

EXTEND THE LEARNING WITH HELICOPTERS: ACTIVITIES

1. **Principles of rotary flight.** Visit http://www.helis.com/howflies/prflight. php. Make at least two more elaborate helicopters using some concepts from this website about rotary flight. Plot the information for each helicopter's flight times, and compare the data according to the following factors:
   - Paper type
   - Wing length
   - Body length
   - Body width
   - Paper clip(s)
   - Fold(s)
   - Taped body and/or wing

   Experiment with varying all of these factors. Use a container as a bull's-eye, and try to land your helicopter on the target. Write a one-page summary of what you have learned about making helicopters.

2. **The Bernoulli Effect.** Daniel Bernoulli, a Swiss scientist who lived during the 18th century, studied the relationship of fluid speed and pressure. He discovered that when a fluid flows through a narrow tube, its speed increases. If you've ever seen a flowing stream, you may have noticed the water's increased speed when it flows through a narrow part.

   The Bernoulli Effect, also known as Bernoulli's Principle, states that fluid must speed up in the constricted region if the flow is to be continuous. Bernoulli figured out that the water got the energy for this extra speed from a lowered internal pressure. The pressure in a fluid decreases as the speed of the fluid increases.

   With regards to flight, this effect is what creates the phenomenon called lift that helps planes fly. A plane that moves through the air has air moving overhead and underneath. The design of airplane wings (called air foils) causes the air on the top of the wing to move faster than the air beneath the wing.

   Visit http://www.physics.umn.edu/outreach/pforce/circus/Bernoulli. html. Conduct one of the experiments described, and then write a one-page summary of your results and how these results reflect the Bernoulli Effect.

Wheelbarrow Races

Build a wheelbarrow to carry the most golf balls a distance of 10 feet.

Subjects and Skills

- Work, force, simple machines
- Circumference
- Measurement conversion
- The history of using simple machines to do work

Materials

- Index cards
- Sturdy paper
- Plastic spoons
- Large buttons
- Paper cups
- Popsicle sticks
- Golf balls

Vocabulary

- Wheelbarrow
- Mural
- Barrow
- Diameter
- Levers
- Wheel
- Axle

Purpose

Understanding the ways in which simple machines (levers and wheel-axle combinations) enable people to use less effort is a fundamental engineering concept. Students will extend their knowledge to the design of Class 2 simple machines and practice the work formula (Work = Force x Distance).

Objectives

Students will gain a better understanding of:
- the history of the wheelbarrow;
- how levers work with axle-wheel combinations to ease exertion;
- converting units of measurement;
- finding circumference of a circle;
- the functionality of the design of the bucket, fulcrum, and wheel; and
- the Work = Force x Distance formula.

Activity Preparation

1. Run off activity sheets.
2. Gather materials and place them in two different areas of the classroom.
3. Bookmark websites to be used in class.
   a. http://vimeo.com/2236446
   b. http://www.mikids.com/SMachinesWheels.htm

Activity Procedure

1. Distribute activity sheets and have students read information.
2. Review the information from the first section of the sheet. Students will sketch wheelbarrows in the space provided and will answer Question 1.
3. Share a video (03:03) at Link a. of a wheelbarrow in action as it is used for carrying baby orangutans after they play in the forest.
4. Ask students to add more information to their responses to Question 1 as they think of ideas.
5. Continue with a discussion on levers and wheel-axle combinations. Ask students to identify examples of the wheel-axle combinations in our world (e.g., bicycles, games, toys, cars). Use Link b. as a resource.
6. Allow students to work on Questions 2 and 3.
7. Review answers to Questions 2 and 3: 6 cubic feet = 10,368 cubic inches; this area would hold 216 bricks (each brick measuring 6" x 4" x 2").
8. Discuss wheel options. Narrow tires are easy to maneuver in small spaces but can be prone to tipping. Wide tires carry heavy loads and suit soft surfaces like lawns, but can be difficult to wheel around narrow paths. Rubber tires are easy to use, soft on gardens, and more versatile.
9. Have students work on Question 6.
10. Review the answer to Question 6. Work = Force (effort) x Distance (time) = (75)(15)(216)(4)= 972,000 N.
11. Ask students to refer back to Question 1. What other ideas did they come up with? Discuss their responses.
12. Write: 16 oz = 1 lb. Ask how many ounces are in 1.5 pounds (24 oz). A golf ball weighs 1.62 ounces. Write this on the board and ask approximately what fraction of a pound this is (approximately 1/10).
13. Put students in groups of two or three, and assign group numbers.
14. Review the team challenge, answering any questions students may have.
15. After the team challenge has been completed, follow up with second set of questions on the activity sheet. To review Questions 1 and 2, circumference = 5.28 in, radius = .84 in., and area = 2.22 sq. in.
16. If you wish, assign one of the projects suggested in Extend the Learning With Wheelbarrows: Activities.

Wheelbarrow Races

GOAL

➢ Build a wheelbarrow to carry the most golf balls 10 feet or further.

MATERIALS

➢ Index cards
➢ Sturdy paper
➢ Plastic spoons
➢ Large buttons

➢ Paper cups
➢ Popsicle sticks
➢ Golf balls

TIME TO CREATE

➢ 20 minutes

INDIVIDUAL ACTIVITY

Read the following, highlighting important information, and then answer the questions.

The wheelbarrow has been around since ancient times. One type of wheelbarrow may have been used in ancient Greece, around 400 B.C., although there is not enough evidence to say so definitively. We do, however, have evidence (from a mural) that wheelbarrows were used during the Han Dynasty (118 A.D.) to transport injured soldiers and supplies. Wheelbarrows originally had two wheels and needed to be moved and steered by two men.

Wheelbarrows did not have their name until the 13th century, when Europeans referred to boards used to transport loads as barrows. When the wheel was added, the barrow became known as a wheelbarrow. A wheelbarrow is a Class 2 machine that uses two simple machines: a lever and a wheel and axle. With a lever, a wheelbarrow helps to lift heavy loads. Levers consist of two effort points and a fulcrum. The wheelbarrow's effort points are the handles and the bucket. The handles are used to lift a load, and the bucket holds the load. The wheel is the fulcrum that allows the wheelbarrow to pivot.

Draw a sketch of a wheelbarrow. Make sure you label the important parts: a bucket to hold the load, a lever to lift the load, and a wheel to transport the load.

Hands-On Engineering © Prufrock Press Inc.

115

Permission is granted to photocopy or reproduce this page for single classroom use only.

1. Wheelbarrows have not changed much in the past 2,000 years, but they still serve an important function in our lives. How do we use wheelbarrows today? _____

   _____

   _____

   _____

   _____

   _____

2. Wheelbarrows allow more goods to be moved in a single trip. If the average wheelbarrow can hold about 6 cubic feet of material, how many cubic inches would that be? _____

3. How many 6" x 4" x 2" bricks could a wheelbarrow hold? (This would be a heavy load, given that each brick weighs about 4 lb.) _____

4. The wheel enables the load to be moved easily and reduces the effort. Thinking about different sizes and types of wheels, how does the radius of the wheel affect the wheelbarrow?

   _____

5. Compare and contrast narrow tires with wide tires. Think about maneuverability, stability, and path surfaces.

   _____

   _____

6. The formula for the relationship between work, necessary force, and distance a load is moved is Work = Force (effort) x Distance (time). Imagine the amount of work you might do on an assignment. If you decrease the force (or effort), you would need to increase the distance (or amount of time) in order to complete the job. It's the same when you are doing physical work. Solve this problem: A 75-pound boy is lifting the bricks from Question 3 and taking them to the construction site 15 meters away. How many Newtons of work will that require?

   _____

   _____

TEAM CHALLENGE

Participants will work together in teams of two or three for 20 minutes to make a sturdy wheelbarrow that travels a distance of at least 10 feet while carrying a load of three or more golf balls. Make sure your team's wheelbarrow is sturdy enough to hold the load and is able to move easily.

When your teacher starts the time, your team will have exactly 20 minutes to gather your materials and build your wheelbarrow. Once the teacher signals that time is up, stop working immediately and bring your wheelbarrow to the challenge site. Any team that continues to work once time is up may be disqualified.

Start Time _____ : _____ + 20 Minutes = _____ : _____ End Time

From a specific starting point, each team will line up with wheelbarrows loaded with the weight. This is not a race. Each team must cross over the finish line with all of its golf balls still safely stored inside the wheelbarrow. If a golf ball escapes from the wheelbarrow, that team will mark that spot as its wheelbarrow's end point. The goal is to have your wheelbarrow carry the greatest weight to the finish line without touching down or spilling its contents.

After the team challenge, answer the following questions.

1. If the diameter of a golf ball is 1.68 inches, then what is the circumference (rounded to the nearest hundredth)? _____

2. What is the golf ball's radius? _____

   What is its area? _____

3. Measure the distance that your team's wheelbarrow traveled. _____

4. How many golf balls was your wheelbarrow able to carry? _____

5. If a golf ball weighs 1.62 oz, how many oz did your wheelbarrow carry? _____

6. Approximately how many pounds is that, rounding to the nearest pound? _____

7. How many golf balls was the most successful wheelbarrow able to carry? _____

8. Expressed in ounces, how much weight was the most successful wheelbarrow able to carry?

   _____

   _____

9. What contributed to whether a wheelbarrow was successful? _____

   _____

   _____

10. What factors hurt some wheelbarrows' performance? _____

    _____

    _____

11. How does the design of the wheelbarrow help with transporting materials?

_____

_____

12. If you were going to make another wheelbarrow, how would you improve on your design?

_____

_____

EXTEND THE LEARNING WITH WHEELBARROWS: ACTIVITIES

1. **Singing about simple machines.** Visit https://vimeo.com/38295614 and https://vimeo.com/38295788 and then write your own song about simple machines. Visit http://www.pbs.org/teachers/connect/resources/3999/preview/?contactID=163798497&gwkey=PFFBPYJTE8 for practice writing lyrics to music. You can write your song in any genre you choose (e.g., pop, rap, classical, country).

2. **Investigating simple machines.** Visit http://teacher.scholastic.com/dirtrep/simple/invest.htm to investigate the facts of simple machines. Complete the observation report and record your findings. Do your work on separate sheets of paper, and turn them in.

3. **Advertising the wheelbarrow.** Videotape (or perform live) a commercial about your wheelbarrow. Learn more about the function of wheelbarrow at http://gomestic.com/gardening/the-function-of-a-wheelbarrow and incorporate new information into your commercial to teach your classmates.

4. **Building a better planet with wheelbarrows.** What else can you do with a wheelbarrow? Check out the experimental solar-powered wheelbarrow at http://creativedynamo.net/faq or http://www.getlofi.com/?p=1184 made from reclaimed waste. DJ Dynamo has created a disco wheelbarrow to take his tunes on the road. Write a news report about this invention and the potential implications for future innovation.

5. **Funky wheelbarrow designs.** Want to try your hand at designing a funky wheelbarrow? Annie has. Check out her funky designs at http://www.funkybarrows.com. Now design your own funky wheelbarrow. Use whatever materials you want, and create a truly funky wheelbarrow. When you're finished, create an ad similar to Annie's ads to sell your wheelbarrow creation. You might even e-mail Annie to share your ideas and make suggestions!

Hands-On Engineering © Prufrock Press Inc.

Permission is granted to photocopy or reproduce this page for single classroom use only.

119

Kite for a Windy Day

Make a kite that will stay aloft for the longest time (at least 3 minutes), with or without weight.

Subjects and Skills
- Kites' history (military, artistic, scientific)
- Gravity, lift
- Surface area, force

Materials
- Sheets of paper or plastic
- Gardening sticks, dowels, or straws
- String or yarn

Vocabulary
- Law of gravity
- Lift
- Force
- Surface area

Purpose
Students will learn how the laws of gravity impact a kite's flying ability.

Objectives
Students will gain a better understanding of:
- Newton's laws of gravity,
- the history of the kite,
- the uses of a kite, and
- surface area.

Activity Preparation
1. Run off activity sheets.
2. Gather materials and place them in two different areas of the room.
3. Bookmark websites to be used in class.
   a. https://vimeo.com/38301007 (show video at http://www.ted.com/talks/saul_griffith_on_kites_as_the_future_of_renewable_energy.html as an extension)
   b. http://kitefestival.com/photo
   c. http://www.grc.nasa.gov/WWW/K-12/airplane/kitefly.html

d. http://www.ehow.com/info_8348108_parts-kite.html

Activity Procedure

1. Introduce kites by showing the video (until the 02:40 mark) from Link a. Stop at the first video stopping point. Ask students if they have ever flown a kite.

2. Show the images available at Link b. Ask questions to foster thinking with depth: How long have kites been around? How have people used kites? How might we use kites to improve the world?

3. Distribute the activity sheets and begin reading and discussing up through Question 2.

4. As a review, ask these questions:
   - Approximately how long have kites been around?
   - Which two countries did kites most likely come from?
   - Who developed the laws of gravitation?
   - In what year did he develop these laws?
   - How old was he when he developed these laws?
   - What is the formula for his second law?

5. Ask why an understanding of kites is important for the future. Begin the video from Link a. starting at 02:40 to have a better understanding of how kites can tap wind energy. Stop at the 04:45 mark. Use the video (05:22) of Saul Griffith's TED Talk, the second site in Link a., as an extension.

6. Discuss the forces that act upon kites. To show the interaction of air pressure with creating lift, use the information at Link c.

7. Review finding the surface area of a kite (1/2 xy, where x is one diagonal and y is the other diagonal). Otherwise put, to find the surface area of a kite, multiply the diagonals and then divide in half. When reviewing students' answers on the activity sheets, for Question 4, the surface area is 150 sq. in.

8. Review the parts of the kite. Use Link d. for students to see the parts on a variety of kites.

9. Review the team challenge and answer any questions that students may have.

10. Once the competition has been completed, have students finish their activity sheets.

11. After reviewing Questions 4–13 and discussing the kite process, show the remainder of the video from Link a. beginning at 04:45.

12. If you wish, organize a fun kite festival by following the guidelines suggested in Extend the Learning With Kites: Teacher Guide to Creating a Kite Festival.

Kite for a Windy Day

Kite for a Windy Day

GOAL

➢ Make a kite that will stay aloft for the longest time (at least 3 minutes), with or without weight.

MATERIALS

➢ Sheets of paper or plastic
➢ Gardening sticks, dowels, or straws
➢ String or yarn

TIME TO CREATE

➢ 20 minutes

INDIVIDUAL ACTIVITY

Read the following, highlighting important information, and then answer the questions.

For more than 2,000 years, people have been flying kites. Whether they have been used to help fight battles, to discover scientific phenomena, to create art, or to transport loads (even people), kites have been instrumental throughout history. Both China and Malaysia are said to have invented the kite. There is evidence to suggest that kites were flown in China as long ago as 200 B.C. to help the Han Dynasty during wars.

In 1666, Isaac Newton developed the laws of gravitation when he was only 23 years old. His first law states that every object will be at rest unless an external force compels it to act. If there is no force, then the object will remain at a velocity of zero. Newton's second law of motion explains how the object's velocity changes when it is subjected to an external force. His law of motion formula is that force is equal to mass multiplied by acceleration, or $F = M \times A$. Newton's third law states that for every action (force), there is an equal and opposite reaction. So, if object A exerts a force on object B, then object B also exerts an equal force on object A. Hold your hands up so they face each other. Your hands are at zero velocity. Now clap your hands one time. Your right hand's force was equal to the force of your left hand.

Similarly, if a gust of wind strikes a kite, then the lift and drag increase. The kite moves higher because the lift exceeds the weight. Kites are able to fly because of the forces acting on the kite.

1. Explain one possible way in which a kite might have been used in war. _____

2. How have kites been helpful in more modern times? _____

_____

_____

3. Without looking at the information that you just read, see how many of your teacher's questions you are able to correctly answer.

4. Even though kites come in different shapes and sizes, forces act the same way on all kites. Similar to an airplane, a kite is a craft that is heavier than air and depends on air pressure for its lift and drag. The surface area of the kite interacts with the wind speed, while the controlled line allows the kite to use the elements to provide the lift. Understanding surface area—the amount of space taken up by all surfaces of the kite—is important to the success of the kite. Find the surface area of a kite with diagonal $x = 20$ inches and diagonal $y = 15$ inches.

_____

5. How might we use kites to channel wind energy?_____

_____

_____

6. A kite has five parts. Draw and label each part.
   a. Frame: keeps kite stiff so it doesn't collapse in wind
   b. Kite covering: material to catch wind and work as a sail
   c. Tail: streamers added to kite to keep it stable
   d. Line: string to hold kite aloft in the wind
   e. Bridle: connects kite to the line to appropriately use the wind

TEAM CHALLENGE

Participants will work together in teams of two or three for 20 minutes to make a kite that will stay aloft for the longest time (at least 3 minutes). You will need to make all five parts of the kite with the materials provided. All teams capable of keeping their kite in the air, without it touching the ground, for at least 3 minutes will be declared victorious, although the longer the kite stays up, the better!

When your teacher starts the time, you will have exactly 20 minutes to gather your materials and build your kite. Once the teacher signals that time is up, stop working immediately and proceed to the challenge site. Any team that continues to work after time has been called may be disqualified.

Hands-On Engineering © Prufrock Press Inc.

123

Permission is granted to photocopy or reproduce this page for single classroom use only.

Complete the following sketch and questions prior to the team challenge. First, draw a sketch of your team's kite and label each part.

```
┌─────────────────────────────────────────┐
│                                         │
│                                         │
│                                         │
│                                         │
│                                         │
│                                         │
│                                         │
│                                         │
│                                         │
│                                         │
└─────────────────────────────────────────┘
```

1. The frame needs to be strong but also lightweight. What is the shape of your kite's frame?

    _____

2. The cover material also needs to be lightweight and strong. What covering or material did you select?_____

3. What is the surface area of your kite's cover? _____

4. What is the length of the stabilizer, or the tail, of the kite? _____

5. How many lines are you using for your kite? _____
    It is important to tie each line to a bridle, or a stick, which are then connected together in the center of the kite. Adjust the lines to direct the angle of the kite for optimum performance.

6. Bowing, either as a smooth curve or an angle at the center of the kite, stabilizes the kite. Bowing can also mean making angles somewhere else on the kite. Did your team bow your kite? _____

7. Venting is when openings are made in the covering material of the kite. Venting allows some air to go through the kite for added stability. Did you add vents? Explain. _____

    _____

After the team challenge, complete the following questions.

1. How long was your kite able to fly? _____

2. What was the record for how long a kite was able to stay in the air? _____

Hands-On Engineering © Prufrock Press Inc.

3. What do you think contributed to the success of a kite's ability to lift into the air and stay aloft? _____

_____

4. What would you do differently if you were making another kite? _____

_____

_____

EXTEND THE LEARNING WITH KITES: TEACHER GUIDE TO CREATING A KITE FESTIVAL

April is National Kite Month, but your class could hold a kite festival in any month. Visit http://www.aka.kite.org/docs/Handbooks/kitc.pdf to see the American Kitefliers Association's *Kites in the Classroom,* a free downloadable handbook of how to incorporate additional learning and workshops about kites into the classroom. If space is an issue, you could hold a miniature festival. Visit http://www.miniaturekiteguild.org to learn more.

1. **Plan the day.** Whether this is schoolwide event or just a special activity for one class, students will embrace the opportunity to become more engaged with kites. All students should be involved in the planning, completing, and reporting of Kite Day. Student roles could include kite designer and flyer, advertiser, planner, and news reporter.

2. **Learn about kite festivals.** Show a couple of kite festival videos at http://www.alivearchives.com. (Click on "Free Kite Movies" and show "What Is a Kite Fest?" and "Kite Man Productions Demo"). Review kite festivals from around the world at Coolum Kite Festival (http://www.coolumkitefestival.com/view_content.asp?ctn_id=25), The World Kite Museum Festival (http://kitefestival.com/kite-festival), and Japanese Kite Festivals (http://www.asahi-net.or.jp/%7Eet3m-tkkw/photogallery.html).

3. **Layer students' understanding about kites.** More information on kites is available at:
    a. How to fly your kite: http://www.gombergkites.com/how.html
    b. Curricular integration: http://www.drachen.org/learn/kite-basics
    c. Information from National Kite Month's site: http://www.national kitemonth.org/main/index.php

4. **Discuss kite classification.** Teach students more about how to classify kites. Topics such as shape, number of lines, material, method for utilizing the air pressure, and more are all interesting elements of kite design. Styles include flat kites, bowed and dihedral kites, cellular and boxed kites, sled kites, parafoil kites, and rotating kites. Visit the following sites for more ideas and information:
    a. http://www.blueskylark.org/zoo/material.html
    b. http://chicagokite.com/stuntkites.html

5. **Select the design.** Have students select their designs, and consider having them explain in writing why they have selected their designs.

6. **Have students advertise.** Students can create advertisements and announcements about the Kite Festival. Posters, videos, articles, and/or announcements will help to inform the community about the event.

7. **Hold the event.** The festival may take anywhere from 1–5 hours, depending on time restraints. One-hour events include the display and flight of the kites, whereas longer events can include specific categories and contests, food and activity booths, and games.

8. **Have students follow up on the event.** Before, during, and after the event, the student news crew will report, via video and written accounts, to document the Kite Festival. The news crew can be responsible for capturing the event on film, as the day will certainly be a colorful and interesting experience! You can come up with further methods for having students reflect on the experience and consider how kites and what they have learned tie into other subjects and applications.

Host a Hoist

Make a hoist that will carry the heaviest load 6 inches from the ground.

Subjects and Skills

- Force, weight, work
- The history of pulleys

Materials

- One paper cup per team
- Plastic spoons
- Dowels or straws
- Spools
- String or yarn
- Cardboard tubing
- Cylindrical containers
- Pennies, marbles, or other weight

Vocabulary

- Archimedes
- Hoist
- Block and tackle
- Reeves
- Sheave

Purpose

Students will learn and apply mechanical engineering concepts regarding how a pulley system changes the force of lifting loads.

Objectives

Students will gain a better understanding of:
- the history of the design of the hoist,
- the mechanics of the block-and-tackle pulley system, and
- changing the force necessary to lift a load.

Activity Preparation

1. Run off activity sheets.
2. Gather materials and place them in two different areas of the room.
3. Bookmark websites to be used in class.
   a. http://www.sacred-destinations.com/greece/meteora-varlaam-monastery

b. http://glencoe.mcgraw-hill.com/sites/0078779626/student_view0/brainpop_movies.html#
c. http://science.howstuffworks.com/transport/engines-equipment/pulley.htm
d. http://library.thinkquest.org/27948/pulley.html
e. http://science.discovery.com/videos/what-the-ancients-knew-force-achimedes-style.html
f. http://www.ffpblog.com/2010/06/a-little-hoist-work
g. http://teachers.egfi-k12.org/lesson-pulleys
h. http://videos.howstuffworks.com/discovery/36077-extreme-engineering-pile-hoisting-video.htm

Activity Procedure

1. Introduce the lesson through images and information of the monastery of St. Barlaam (also called Varlaam monastery) at Link a. Ask students to imagine building the monastery in the 15th century. How did the builders get to the location? How were materials carried up the peak? How might we build it today?
2. Distribute the activity sheet to read and discuss it together.
3. After reading the second paragraph, show the video on pulleys available at Link b.
4. As students complete Question 1, share information available at Link c. to explain how the block and tackle works, along with information at Link d. to show how the pulley works.
5. Show What the Ancients Knew: Force—Archimedes style (01:17) at Link e. to layer students' understanding of how the force of the weight is changed by using a pulley.
6. After students discuss Question 2 on the activity sheet (other uses for hoist systems), share the journal of a combat medic at Link f.
7. Show and discuss whale transport as discussed at Link g.
8. While students complete Question 3 on the activity sheet, put students into groups of two or three and assign group numbers.
9. Review the team challenge, answering any questions that students may have.
10. After the challenge has been conducted, have students complete their activity sheets.
11. Show the video (02:13) about extreme engineering at Link h.
12. If you wish, assign one of the activities suggested in Extend the Learning With Hoists: Activities.

Host a Hoist

Host a Hoist

GOAL

➤ Make a hoist that will carry the heaviest load 6 inches from the ground.

MATERIALS

➤ One paper cup per team
➤ Plastic spoons
➤ Dowels or straws
➤ Spools

➤ String or yarn
➤ Cardboard tubing
➤ Cylindrical containers
➤ Pennies, marbles, or other weight

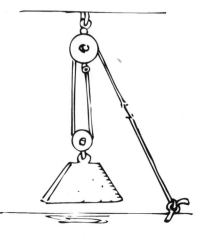

TIME TO CREATE

➤ 20 minutes

INDIVIDUAL ACTIVITY

Read the following, highlight important information, and then answer the questions.

The pulley-hoist system has enabled people, animals, and water power to lift large loads with little force for thousands of years. Archimedes (approximately 287–212 B.C.), the most famous ancient Greek mathematician and inventor, developed the pulley to be used against Rome. His design included a pulley attached to a lever with a giant hook at the end. When Roman ships approached, the pulley would be lowered over a wall, hook the ships, lift them out of the water, and then drop them to the ground, crushing them.

Pulleys, operated by ropes, make it possible to hoist—or lift—heavy objects. The ropes are coiled around a grooved wheel, which creates a change to the mechanical force enabling objects to be lifted over a vertical path. A block-and-tackle heavy is an apparatus of pulleys and ropes used for hauling and hoisting heavy objects. Pulleys are often incorporated into the design of engineering systems such as the crane or the hoist. Hoists are mechanisms that use a pulley system to change the distribution of the force necessary to lift and lower a suspended load.

The Greek monastery of St. Barlaam is an impressive example of how hoists can help to accomplish amazing feats. The monastery sits atop a peak 200 feet above the ground, and the only way to get materials there was by using a hoist. Imagine how many pounds were lifted over the course of building the monastery!

The hoist's design eventually led to the invention of elevators. In 1853, American inventor Elisha Otis demonstrated the first elevator. Multiple wire ropes attached to the top of the elevator car help to raise and lower the car. The wires are coiled around sheaves (grooved wheels or pulleys) and are attached to a weight at the other end. Otis's name is synonymous with elevators even today.

1. Draw a sketch of how a hoist, using a pulley system, is able to change the force required to lift a load. Use the terms below to label the parts.
   - ➤ Crane: a mechanism used to lift and lower loads.
   - ➤ Reeves or chain fall lines: lines between the hoist body and the bottom hook.
   - ➤ Lift: the maximum distance the bottom hook can travel.
   - ➤ Sheave: a pulley used with a chain or wire rope hoist.

2. By lifting materials and moving products from one location to another, hoists play a vital role in construction. What are other uses for hoists? _____
   _____
   _____

3. With the available materials, what might you use for each of these parts as your team designs and builds a hoist?

   Reeves: _____

   Crane: _____

   Sheave: _____

TEAM CHALLENGE

Participants will work together in teams of two or three for 20 minutes to make a hoist that will lift the heaviest load 6 inches off the ground. The team whose hoist lifts the heaviest load wins. As an additional challenge, try to build a hoist that will be able to transport the load from side to side.

As you design the pulley, think about the following:
- ➤ The support to hang the pulley from must be stabile.
- ➤ The location of where you stand needs to allow you to pull the rope freely and draw in the slack.
- ➤ You must be able to pull the basket up slowly and steadily to the appropriate height.
- ➤ To suspend the basket at a certain height, the rope must be tied to a counterweight or anchor.

Once the teacher starts the time, your team will have exactly 20 minutes to design and build your hoist. Once the teacher signals that time is up, you must stop working immediately and proceed to the challenge site. Any team that continues to work after time has been called may be disqualified.

Start Time _____ : _____ + 20 Minutes = _____ : _____ End Time

After the team challenge, answer the following questions.

1. What was the maximum weight your hoist was able to handle? _____

2. How did your team stabilize the basket carrying the load? _____

3. What modifications did you or would you make to enable a hoist to move a load horizontally as well as vertically? _____

_____

_____

4. Were you, or was any other team, able to build a hoist that was also able to carry the load from side to side? _____

5. What uses could this serve? _____

6. What was the maximum load a team's hoist was able to carry? _____

7. What contributed to the success of the design of the most successful hoist? _____

_____

_____

8. If you had access to any material, what would be the strongest material for the reeves?

_____

_____

9. What changes would you make to your team's design to improve the hoist? _____

_____

_____

_____

EXTEND THE LEARNING WITH HOISTS: ACTIVITIES

1. **Fixed pulleys, moveable pulleys, and two-pulley systems.** Learn about a variety of types of pulleys by visiting http://www.the-office.com/summerlift/pulleybasics.htm. For more information on the types of pulleys, go to http://www.newworldencyclopedia.org/entry/Pulley or http://www.technologystudent.com/gears1/pulley8.htm. A fixed pulley is attached to a structure. A flagpole is an example of a fixed pulley. A moveable pulley is a pulley attached to a moving object. A construction crane is an example of a moveable pulley. Think of more uses for different types of pulleys. Write about two of your ideas, and draw pictures with labels.

2. **Mechanical advantage.** Visit http://library.thinkquest.org/CR0210120/Mechanical%20Advantage.html. What is the efficiency of a pulley system when its work out equals 100 Joules, and its work in equals 150 Joules? Mechanical advantage is the degree to which a machine helps a person do his or her work, expressed as a ratio. The larger the mechanical advantage, the easier the work is. The formula for mechanical advantage is resistance force divided by effort force. Research the mechanical advantage of other pulleys, and share what you learned in a couple of paragraphs.

3. **In-depth mechanical advantage.** How can the effectiveness of a system of pulleys be measured? By calculating the mechanical advantage, we can measure the effectiveness of a pulley system. The mechanical advantage of all simple machines is defined by a mathematical expression. When working with pulleys, the most precise method for calculating the mechanical advantage is by counting the number of ropes that support the load. The mathematical expression for the mechanical advantage of a pulley is:

$$\text{Mechanical advantage} = \left[\frac{\text{Input distance (weight of load)}}{\text{Output distance (number of ropes)}}\right] = \frac{\text{Number of ropes}}{\text{supporting load}}$$

   Go to http://www.the-office.com/summerlift/pulleybasics.htm for visuals of the ropes. When you feel ready, practice calculating the pulley's mechanical advantage. Visit http://www.swe.org/iac/lp/pulley_act.html and http://www.dynamicscience.com.au/tester/solutions/hydraulicus/pulleys3.htm for practice.

4. **Real-world application.** Look for pulleys around you. Record the information in the table below. Share the results, and summarize what you learned in a paragraph.

PULLEYS IN MY WORLD

Pulley	Number of Ropes	Force Applied	Length of Rope	Mechanical Advantage

Obstacle Course, of Course

Make an obstacle course for a marble that will have a minimum of three actions. All teams that design a successful three-action obstacle course will be declared victorious!

Subjects and Skills

- Mechanical force
- Potential energy, kinetic energy

Materials

- Shoe boxes
- Cardboard tubing
- Paper
- Popsicle sticks
- Dowels
- Straws
- String, yarn, or twine
- Paper cups
- Plastic spoons
- Marbles
- Coffee containers
- Egg cartons
- Film canisters
- Play dough/clay

Vocabulary

- Cause and effect
- Potential energy
- Kinetic energy
- Mechanical force
- Friction
- Gravity
- Lever

Purpose

Students will apply the engineering concepts associated with simple machines and the ideas of mechanical force and kinetic and potential energy by designing an obstacle course. An understanding of how mechanical engineering principles come together to create cause and effect is essential to design.

Objectives

Students will gain a better understanding of the applications of:

- simple machines,
- mechanical engineering,
- kinetic and potential energy,
- Newton's Laws, and
- the cause and effect of mechanical actions.

Activity Preparation

1. Run off activity sheets.
2. Gather materials and place them in two different areas in the classroom.
3. Bookmark websites to be used in class.
   a. http://www.engineeringinteract.org/interact.htm
   b. http://www.funderstanding.com/k12/coaster
   c. http://glencoe.mcgraw-hill.com/sites/0078779626/student_view0/
      brainpop_movies.html#
   d. http://www.pbs.org/media/wgbh/designsquad/animations/301_
      lever_hi.mov
   e. http://thestir.cafemom.com/big_kid/100151/ok_go_video_like_
      mouse

Activity Procedure

1. Review forces using the information at Link a. To save time, you may want to assign the activities on this site as homework or complete them during a computer lab lesson. Important scientific concepts reviewed through the site include gravity, friction, compression, stretching, Newtons, air resistance, balanced and unbalanced forces, Newton's laws of motion, magnetic forces, attraction and repulsion, magnetic metals, and the pulley system.
2. Distribute the activity sheets and have students read the first paragraph.
3. Show the interactive roller coaster at Link b. This site will demonstrate the effects of changing the size of the loop, the speed of the coaster, the coaster's mass, the gravity at work, and the amount of friction on the track. If time allows, provide an opportunity for students to practice on their own, whether with homework, a computer lab, a class computer, small groups, or whatever other method works best for your classroom and schedule.
4. Allow time for students to respond to Questions 1–3, and then discuss answers.

5. Ask students to explain kinetic and potential energy. An excellent source for a quick review is available at Link c. Scroll to the bottom for a kinetic energy video (02:23) and a potential energy video (02:03).

6. Allow time for students to complete Questions 4–6, and then discuss answers, which are as follow:
   - Potential Energy is **the stored energy** of an object due to its **position** or **condition**.
   - Kinetic energy is the energy that an object has due to **its motion**. Kinetic energy depends on the **mass** and **speed** of an object.
   - Kinetic energy is transferred from one object to another when **they collide**.

7. Have students balance pencils on their index fingers. Introduce or review the term *lever* (a rod with a pivot point). Demonstrate what happens if you have a pencil balanced on your finger and you tap one end. If you allow students to practice, be careful about how close they are sitting to one another. Show the clip on how levers work at Link d. Discuss and allow time for students to complete Question 7, and then discuss the answers (greater, farther, pivot point, faster).

8. Review the available materials and supplies for the challenge with students, and then allow them time to complete Questions 8–10.

9. If time allows, have students briefly share their ideas.

10. If you are spreading out this challenge over a couple of days, you might allow students to complete Questions 8–10 at home. When you return to the challenge, briefly review the work and continue on to the challenge.

11. Assign teams and team numbers.

12. Review the challenge and address any questions that students may have.

13. After the challenge has been completed, review the teams' processes and have students complete Questions 1–5.

14. Show a video (03:54) at Link e. of an elaborate obstacle course set to music with unique cause-and-effect mechanisms that result in the group being spray painted. Students of all ages will love this!

15. If you wish, use Extend the Learning With Obstacle Courses: Building a Bigger, Better Course to allow students to construct more advanced obstacle courses. This could be an out-of-class activity, or you could devote additional class time to allowing students to incorporate higher level components into their obstacle courses.

Obstacle Course, of Course

Obstacle Course, of Course

GOAL

➢ Make an obstacle course for a marble that will have a minimum of three actions. All teams that design a successful three-action obstacle course will be declared victorious!

MATERIALS

➢ Shoe boxes
➢ Cardboard tubing
➢ Paper
➢ Popsicle sticks
➢ Dowels
➢ Straws
➢ String, yarn, or twine

➢ Paper cups
➢ Plastic spoons
➢ Marbles
➢ Coffee containers
➢ Egg cartons
➢ Film canisters
➢ Play dough/clay

TIME TO CREATE

➢ 30 minutes

INDIVIDUAL ACTIVITY

Read the following, highlighting important information, and then answer the questions.

You've learned about the scientific physics concepts of force, motion, inertia, gravity, friction, and balance. Now you're going to apply these ideas in the design of an obstacle course for a marble. You will want to use gravity to help the marble move. Understanding how kinetic energy works with potential energy will help your team use other objects to create a cause-and-effect path for the marble to transfer from one action to another. When designing your obstacle course, you will include a series of tubes, tracks, lifts, hoists, and other modes to enable the marble to go from one point to another.

In thinking about kinetic and potential energy, you'll want to strategically place objects to change the marble's direction or affect the marble's speed. By using kinetic and potential energy, the marble will stay on track and transfer from one location to another.

Designing your obstacle course to include a minimum of three actions will require you to think about the causes and effects of mechanical engineering options. Engineers must think about the relationships of one action and another.

1. How does the size of a loop affect the velocity of an object? _____

2. How does the mass of an object affect its speed?_____

3. How does friction affect an object? _____

4. Potential Energy is _____ of an object due to

   its _____ ,

   or _____ .

5. Kinetic energy is the energy that an object has due to _____ .

   Kinetic energy depends on the _____

   and _____ of an object.

6. Kinetic energy is transferred from one object to another when _____ .

7. Levers also help move objects. How does the placement of the pivot point affect the object's

   movement? The longer the arm is, the _____ the distance is that

   must be traveled, because it's _____ from

   the _____ . In terms of speed, this will make the object

   move _____ .

8. Think about different engineering actions you want to include in your obstacle course for your

   marble to travel. Make a list of three different ideas.

   a. _____

   b. _____

   c. _____

9. Friction can cause the marble to slow down when necessary. There are different ways to create friction in your team's obstacle course. Name a couple of ways in which you might create
   friction, with the available supplies, for your team's marble. _____

   _____

   _____

10. What types of actions and reactions do you want to include in your obstacle course? List three
    or more actions and decide which available supplies might provide the desired result in your
    team's obstacle course. This will take some thought. List the action, the reaction, and the
    supplies needed.

    a. _____

    b. _____

    c. _____

TEAM CHALLENGE

Participants will work together in teams of two or three for 30 minutes to make an obstacle course with at least three actions. Using any of the materials provided, construct an obstacle course for a marble that will have a minimum of three actions. Once the marble is released at the starting point, a minimum of three separate actions will take place before the marble reaches the finish. Share and review each team member's ideas (listed previously on this activity sheet), and decide which ones you will incorporate into your team's design, perhaps with modifications.

List the actions that you will include in your obstacle course below. These actions will be the plan for your team's obstacle course. List the item, the action, and the reaction.

1. _____

   _____

2. _____

   _____

3. _____

   _____

Work together to design the obstacle course, keeping in mind that you have limited time, and that everybody's contributions are valuable. Once the teacher starts the time, you will have exactly 30 minutes to design an obstacle course and build it. Once the teacher signals that time is up, stop working immediately. Any team that continues to work after the time has been called may be disqualified.

> Start Time _____ : _____ + 30 Minutes = _____ : _____ End Time

After the team challenge, answer the following questions.

1. Which action from your obstacle course was your favorite? Explain why._____

   _____

   _____

   _____

2. Of all of the other obstacle courses, which action was your favorite? Describe the material used and the action that occurred. _____

   _____

   _____

   _____

3. Explain one action, either from your team's or another team's course, that did not accomplish the intended goal. _____

_____

_____

4. What could have been done differently to prevent the action's failure? _____

_____

_____

_____

5. Think of another material that could have been provided that might have added to your obstacle course. Describe the item and the action. _____

_____

_____

_____

EXTEND THE LEARNING WITH OBSTACLE COURSES: CREATING A BIGGER, BETTER COURSE

Work with another student or as a class to design a bigger, better obstacle course. You may use whatever materials you like, as long as you do not purchase anything new. All materials must be recycled from other sources. Keep in mind that the only time you touch the obstacle course can be to initiate the sequence of actions. The longer the marble takes to move through the obstacle course, the better. The rules are:

◆ All motion of the object must be created indirectly through changing the position, velocity, or acceleration of the course. No one may touch the object once it has been set in motion.

◆ Once your object is in the "starting block," it can receive no outside assistance.

◆ The object may not leave the course at any time.

◆ The obstacle course must be portable (multiple people may carry the course, but it will need to be moveable).

◆ You may make a motorized control system, but you may not purchase one.

◆ The course must be safe for users and spectators.

◆ You will have 10 minutes on the day of the competition to set up and perform the obstacle course.

◆ You may have as many attempts to operate the course successfully as you like within 10 minutes.

◆ Adults or older students may not complete any component of the design or construction of the course.

The obstacle course will be scored according to the following guidelines:

◆ Each action earns 5 points.

◆ Each mechanical concept earns 5 points.

◆ Each second that the object is in motion, from beginning to end, earns 1 point .

◆ Each unique idea that no other team has used will earn 5 points.

◆ Any other point guidelines and grading criteria set by the teacher apply.

Craft a Raft

Make a raft with a sail that will stay afloat for at least 1 minute while carrying the heaviest load.

Subjects and Skills

- The relationship between buoyancy and density
- The history (interdisciplinary) of rafts

Materials

- Sheets of plastic
- Fabric scraps
- Foil
- Egg cartons
- Jar lids
- Straws
- Popsicle sticks
- Twine
- Clay
- Large basin of water, sink, fountain, or kiddie pool

Vocabulary

- Buoyancy
- Density

Purpose

Students will understand the relationship of buoyancy and density through applying skills. Students will learn about rafting through a combination of literature and physics.

Objectives

Students will gain a better understanding of:
- the history of the design of the raft,
- Mark Twain's settings for *The Adventures of Tom Sawyer* and *The Adventures of Huckleberry Finn*,
- designing and engineering a raft to stay afloat while carrying a load, and
- applying buoyancy and density calculations.

Activity Preparation

1. Run off activity sheets.
2. Gather materials and place them in two different areas of the room.

Craft a Raft

3. Bookmark websites to be used in class.
    a. https://vimeo.com/27603039
    b. http://dsc.discovery.com/videos/mythbusters-lets-talk-buoyancy.html
    c. http://www.pbs.org/wgbh/nova/lasalle/buoybasics.html
    d. http://vimeo.com/26932507

Activity Procedure

1. Show the raft video (03:17) at Link a. as an exciting introduction to rafting. Allow for a 2-minute think-pair-share discussion about the video.
2. Explain that the students will be designing a raft for their team challenge. Ask what students remember about buoyancy from the boat challenge, or review other concepts you've covered in class (buoyancy and density). Archimedes' principle states that an object's ability to float depends on upward force, or displacement, of water against the object. An object's ability to float depends on the density, or weight per unit of volume, of the body compared to the fluid; this determines the buoyant force. The boat's hull must have a mass that, when divided by its volume, will provide a density equal the amount of water displaced.
3. Show the video (03:13) at Link b. For additional review, go to Link c.
4. Distribute the activity sheets. Ask if any students have read or heard of Samuel Langhorne Clemens. Explain that his pen name was Mark Twain, and he wrote *The Adventures of Tom Sawyer* (1876) and *The Adventures of Huckleberry Finn* (1884).
5. After students complete Question 4, discuss their responses for Questions 1–4.
6. Show the video (02:15) about raft plans available at Link d. Discuss specific ideas generated from the video.
7. Students will continue reading the information. Review their responses for Questions 4–10. Their answer to Question 9 should include information indicating that the mass, when divided by the volume, will provide a density equal the amount of water displaced.
8. Review the team challenge, answering any questions students may have. Put students into groups and assign group numbers. Hold the challenge in whatever manner is most convenient and appropriate for your classroom.
9. Have students complete their activity sheets once the team challenge has been completed.
10. If you wish, use Extend the Learning With Rafts: Teacher's Guide to a Choose Your Own Adventure Unit to lead students in furthering their exploration of rafts and literature.

Craft a Raft

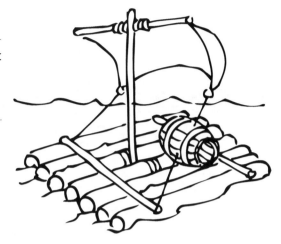

GOAL

➢ Make a raft with a sail that will stay afloat for at least 1 minute while carrying the heaviest load.

MATERIALS

➢ Sheets of plastic
➢ Fabric scraps
➢ Foil
➢ Egg cartons
➢ Jar lids

➢ Straws
➢ Popsicle sticks
➢ Twine
➢ Clay

TIME TO CREATE

➢ 20 minutes

INDIVIDUAL ACTIVITY

Read the following, highlight important information, and then answer the questions.

Samuel Langhorne Clemens, a famous author known as Mark Twain, was born in Missouri in 1835. As a young adult, Clemens became a riverboat pilot and spent many years on the Mississippi River. Life on the river provided him with much of the material he would later use for adventurous raft scenes in two of his most famous novels, *The Adventures of Tom Sawyer* (1876) and *The Adventures of Huckleberry Finn* (1884).

Rafts have served as an inexpensive mode of water transportation since ancient times. Civilizations often developed near rivers, and rafts made it easier to transport materials for building and trading from one site to another. During ancient times, rafts were typically made of lumber, reeds, and/or animal skin. Today's raft designs are quite different.

1. What material do we use today when building a raft? _____

2. Where might you see a raft today? _____

3. How are people able to manually (without a motor) steer rafts? _____

4. What elements are important in designing and building a raft? _____

_____

_____

5. Many of Twain's stories depict a sense of freedom as Tom and Huck run away and drift down the Mississippi River toward a new, unknown life. Imagine living and traveling on a raft.

Hands-On Engineering © Prufrock Press Inc.

145

Permission is granted to photocopy or reproduce this page for single classroom use only.

Design a raft that you would be able to live on for 1 week. Include realistic ideas. You will not have access to electricity, nor will you be able to stop off at places to pick up materials or supplies.

```


```

6. The three main types of rafts are rafts that are steered with a paddle at the stern, rafts that are controlled by rudders, and rafts with central helms (oars). How will your raft be steered during the time when you are asleep? _____

7. What would you pack for a weeklong rafting adventure? _____

8. How would you control the raft's speed? _____

   _____

   _____

9. How does the raft's hull prevent it from sinking? _____

   _____

   _____

10. If you built your raft on land, how would you transport it to the water? _____

TEAM CHALLENGE

Participants will work together in teams of two or three for 20 minutes to make a raft with a sail that is able to float while carrying the maximum load afloat for at least 1 minute.

Once the teacher starts the time, your team will have exactly 20 minutes to gather materials and build your raft. Once the teacher signals that time is up, you must stop working immediately and proceed to the challenge site. Any team that continues to work after time is up may be disqualified.

After the team challenge, answer the following questions.

1. How much weight was your team's raft able to hold? _____

2. What design elements does a raft need to be successful? _____

3. What material(s) would be best for constructing a raft, and why? _____

4. What was the class record for the heaviest load held by a raft? _____

5. If you were able to build your team's raft to a scale of 1 mm = 5 m, would you be able to survive on your raft living on a river for a week? Explain what would need to be done to your raft to allow for you to live more comfortably and safely for 1 week. _____

_____

_____

_____

_____

EXTEND THE LEARNING WITH RAFTS: TEACHER'S GUIDE TO A CHOOSE YOUR OWN ADVENTURE UNIT

Overview

Choose Your Own Adventure is a collaborative writing style. Students will work with partners or in small groups to write a Choose Your Own Adventure book.

Students will also each contribute a second-person point of view story about a river rafting adventure. Once students have completed these, each story may be a part of a class book in which the reader assumes the role of the protagonist. The protagonist makes decisions that determine the main character's actions, thus determining the outcome of the plot.

Lessons

Lesson 1: Introducing Choose Your Own Adventure

Begin by introducing the Choose Your Own Adventure story type. Several sites offer examples of Choose Your Own Adventure stories; search for a couple that are appropriate for your students. (You might try WritingFix, TeacherVision, and ReadWriteThink.)

Once students understand the basic concept of this type of adventure story, return to the setting of the river. Discuss various river settings for students' stories. Each story may include multiple settings for the reader to experience. For example, one story may begin with the reader making a decision between the Nile and the Colorado rivers. There are more than 200 famous rivers and more than 1,000,000 named rivers around the world for students to include in their settings. Students will investigate rivers and narrow their results to 10 rivers, each from a different country. You could use this as an opportunity to have students do more in-depth independent research, if you wish.

Lesson 2: Learning About Point of View and Other Literary Elements

Teach or review the elements of fiction: setting, character development, plot structure, conflict, and point of view. Choose Your Own Adventure is written from a second-person point of view, using "you" as the viewpoint. (For example, "You take a deep breath and close your eyes. Navigating through the rapids is

Hands-On Engineering © Prufrock Press Inc.

going to require all of your strength; however, you have a sinking feeling that you might not be able to win the battle today.") Students will practice writing second-person point of view statements and paragraphs.

Lesson 3: Organizing the Story

Organizing the story will work best if students work with partners or in small groups. Graphic organizers are excellent tools for students to plan out the first part of the story. Multiple sites offer a variety of graphic organizers to choose from, including the Education Place, Freeology, and TeacherVision.

Students will continue planning and writing each part of their story until they have established the setting, characters, exposition (detailed description), and narrative hook.

Lesson 4: Developing the Storyline

Students should continue developing the story through plot development leading to rising action and conflict (two more paths). The story will continue to the climax, and then will be resolved. Students' stories should allow for a total of four possible conclusions.

As the students progress through the completion of their stories, plan on multiple opportunities for students to meet and discuss their story contributions with their group.

Lesson 5: Editing and Publishing

Each group will edit and revise its story. The final story will be published through an available website. By gaining an audience, students take themselves and their work more seriously. You can use The WritersSite's list of online publishing tools at http://www.thewriterssite.com/direct_pages/online_resources.html for ideas.

Lesson 6: Reflecting on the Work

Self-reflection allows students to think about the story-writing process and evaluate their performance according to their writing abilities, effort, and collaboration skills.

Students will think about their contributions and finish the following statements:

1. In terms of my writing abilities:
   - I was most proud of . . .
   - Something new that I tried was . . .
   - An area of growth that I noticed was . . .
   - A new writing goal for me to work on is . . .

Hands-On Engineering © Prufrock Press Inc.

Permission is granted to photocopy or reproduce this page for single classroom use only.

149

2. In terms of my collaboration skills:
   - ◆ I was most proud of . . .
   - ◆ Something new that I tried was . . .
   - ◆ An area of growth that I noticed was . . .
   - ◆ A new collaboration goal for me to work on is . . .
   - ◆ One positive lesson I learned from working with others was . . .

Additional Lesson Resources

Graphic Organizers
- ◆ http://www.eduplace.com/graphicorganizer/
- ◆ http://freeology.com/graphicorgs
- ◆ http://www.teachervision.fen.com/graphic-organizers/printable/6293.html
- ◆ http://interactives.mped.org/view_interactive.aspx?id=127&title

Examples of Choose Your Own Adventure Stories
- ◆ http://writingfix.com/Chapter_Book_Prompts/CYOA3.htm
- ◆ http://www.teachervision.fen.com/creative-writing/activity/3139.html
- ◆ http://www.angelfire.com/wy/lemmingpie/redwallcyoa.html

CD Car

Make a car that will travel the furthest while carrying weight.

Subjects and Skills
- Circumference, area
- Velocity, mass, force

Materials
- Paper
- Cardboard tubing
- Straws
- String, yarn, or twine
- Four CDs or other disc-shaped objects per team
- Paper plates
- Paper bowls
- Plastic spoons
- Ramp, slanted board, or nearby hill

Vocabulary
- Combustion
- Internal combustion
- External combustion

Purpose

Engineering and design often require applying principles of a specific design to another purpose. Students will learn how Karl Benz applied the concepts of the bicycle to combustion to invent the first self-powered automobile used for personal travel.

Objectives

Students will learn about and understand:
- how engineers used the principles of the wheel design to improve transportation's efficiency,
- the first three-wheeled automobile (optional),
- how internal and external combustion work to generate usable energy, and
- how the circumference and area of a circle are applied to solve real-world problems.

Activity Preparation

1. Run off activity sheets.
2. Gather materials and place them in two different areas in the classroom.
3. Bookmark websites to be used in class.
   a. http://vimeo.com/26898353
   b. http://www.history.com/shows/modern-marvels/videos/who-invented-the-wheel#who-invented-the-wheel
   c. http://www.howstuffworks.com/engine.htm
   d. http://www.pitara.com/discover/5wh/online.asp?story=28
   e. https://vimeo.com/26894196

Activity Procedure

1. As a hook for the lesson, show a video (00:48) of the invention of the Dynasphere at Link a.
2. Ask students to think about these questions: Who invented the wheel? When was it invented? How has the wheel changed the way we live?
3. Distribute the activity sheets. Students will read and highlight information and write responses. After students have responded to the first three questions, review and discuss their responses.
4. Discuss ideas from the video "Who Invented the Wheel?" (01:39) at Link b. The wheel was invented around 3,000 B.C. in ancient Mesopotamia. The addition of the wheel to the farmers' carts allowed for crops to be moved to cities. The discovery of rotary motion occurred around 8,000 B.C. The uses of the wheel were helpful in everyday tasks. Pulleys made lifting heavy stones easier. Water wheels helped to generate power. Rotating gears became essential for a variety of tools.
5. Introduce the term *combustion*. Combustion is the process that takes place when oxygen atoms, heat, and a fuel source react with each other. Combustion is also called burning. For a video (01:38) on combustion, go to Link c. For information on the steam engine, visit Link d.
6. After the students learn about the steam engine, use the video (01:11) at Link e. to introduce Karl Benz's three-wheeled tricycle.
7. As students finish the independent activity, assign teams and team numbers. Review area and circumference of circles (if necessary) and review the team challenge, answering any questions that students may have.
8. Once 20 minutes have elapsed, direct students to move to a ramp, a slanted board, or a nearby hill with their CD cars for the challenge. Whatever setup you use, you will have to allow enough space for the cars to travel as far as they can, so the area after the incline will have to be cleared.
9. After the challenge, have students complete their activity sheets.
10. If you wish, assign an activity suggested in Extend the Learning With Cars: Activities.

CD Car

GOAL

> ➤ Make a car that will travel the furthest while carrying weight.

MATERIALS

> ➤ Paper
> ➤ Cardboard tubing
> ➤ Straws
> ➤ Four CDs or other disc-shaped objects per team

> ➤ Plastic spoons
> ➤ Paper plates
> ➤ Paper bowls
> ➤ String, yarn, or twine

TIME TO CREATE

> ➤ 20 minutes

INDIVIDUAL ACTIVITY

Read the following passage, highlighting important information, and then answer the questions.

With the invention of the wheel—which occurred, according to archeologists, in about 6000 B.C. by the Sumerians—the concept of a more efficient mode of transportation took hold. For thousands of years, our fascination with transportation has led us through water, land, air, and space. In the late 15th century, Leonardo da Vinci introduced sketches of a self-powered vehicle. At that time, a self-powered vehicle was a rather farfetched concept.

It didn't come to pass until 1705, when Thomas Newcomen invented the first engine powered by combustion (a chemical process of burning fuel that occurs when a fuel substance reacts with oxygen in the air to give off heat). Newcomen's engine was known as the steam engine, as it was an external combustion engine that converted steam into energy. The steam engine's fuel burned outside of the engine to create steam, which created motion inside of the engine. The steam engine powered all early locomotives, steamboats, and factories.

The first steam-driven tractor, introduced in the 1760s, was built as a means of transporting a cannon. The tractor was a large, three-wheeled vehicle capable of traveling at speeds of approximately 3 miles per hour, which isn't much faster than the pace at which a person walks.

Internal combustion is smaller and more efficient than external combustion, and it takes less fuel per mile. In 1885, German inventor Karl Benz produced the first three-wheeled vehicle powered by an internal combustion engine.

1. Who most likely invented the wheel?_____

2. List some ways we use wheels today. _____

_____

Hands-On Engineering © Prufrock Press Inc.

153

Permission is granted to photocopy or reproduce this page for single classroom use only.

3. Over the past couple of centuries, what sources have been utilized to enable vehicles to move? _____

4. About how fast can an automobile travel today?_____

5. If wheeled vehicles had not been invented, how might students go to and from school each day?_____

   _____

   _____

6. Leonardo da Vinci saw ways that machines could save people time and effort, and he used his creativity and his understanding of machinery to design and sketch his inventions. You are going to design a vehicle of your own. Draw a sketch of what your CD car might look like, labeling specific parts.

7. Look at what materials will be available to you during this challenge. Write into your sketch what materials you will use for each part.

8. Wheels are circular. Write the formulas for finding the area and circumference of a circle.

   Area: _____

   Circumference:_____

9. Find the area and circumference, rounded to the nearest hundredth, of a wheel with a 5-inch radius: A = _____ C = _____

TEAM CHALLENGE

Participants will work together in teams of two or three for 20 minutes to design and build a car that will travel the furthest distance while carrying weight. Each team can incorporate elements of each team member's individual designs, if desired.

When the teacher starts the time, your group will have exactly 20 minutes to gather your materials and build your car. Once the teacher signals that time is up, stop working immediately and proceed with your car to the challenge site. Any team that continues working after the time is up may be disqualified.

Start Time _____ : _____ + 20 Minutes = _____ : _____ End Time

After the team challenge has been completed, answer the following questions.

1. Sketch and label your team's car.

2. Record the distance, time, and weight of five different cars. Evaluate the results and write a brief analysis of each car's performance specific to the strengths and weaknesses.

Team #	Distance in Inches	Time in Seconds	Weight	Analysis

3. Which car was able to travel the furthest with the most weight?_____

4. What do you think contributed to the success of the car that was able to carry a load the furthest? _____

    _____

    _____

5. If you were going to build a car capable of transporting a person, what materials would you use?_____

    _____

    _____

6. How would the car move? _____

    _____

    _____

7. How might cars change over the next 25–50 years? _____

    _____

    _____

EXTEND THE LEARNING WITH CARS: ACTIVITIES

1. **Explore cars' effects on the environment.** With soaring gas prices and concerns for air quality, it has become necessary to investigate alternative fuels for our cars. CNN has dedicated coverage to enlightening Americans on the impact of our oil consumption. Research a variety of articles and videos by visiting http://www.cnn.com/SPECIALS/2008/fueling.america, and complete a report on alternative fuels. Select a topic to report on from the information, and then act as a video journalist to create a news report. Your analysis should include comparisons of miles per gallon for various cars. Your purpose is to educate others to use public transportation and/or alternative fuels as a resource.

2. **Make a persuasive speech or report about alternative fuels.** Conduct research and then summarize what you have learned about what must be done to make a positive change. For compelling facts, review the U.S. Department of Energy's statistics on alternative fuels at http://www.afdc.energy.gov/afdc/fuels. You can also visit the following websites to gather information:
   - http://www.pbs.org/newshour/indepth_coverage/science/alt_fuels/
   - http://www.energyquest.ca.gov/transportation/biodiesel.html

3. **Design the car of the future.** Visit http://www.pbs.org/wgbh/nova/tech/car-of-the-future.html, a powerful NOVA presentation (53:12) about two brothers' journey to make a car of the future. Continue to the Model of Efficiency at http://www.pbs.org/wgbh/nova/car/efficiency.html. Learn about the changes in car design, materials, safety, weight, software, functionality, aerodynamics, air drag, style, tires, speed, accessories propulsion, fuels, internal combustion, biodiesel, and concept cars from real-life car companies (e.g., Toyota, Nissan, Mazda). Design your own car of the future, and write a page about the elements of your car that make it an improvement over current vehicles.

It's Getting Hot in Here

Make a solar oven that cooks an egg the fastest.

Subjects and Skills
- Greenhouse effect
- Measuring temperature
- Calculating volume

Materials
- Cardboard
- Foil
- Plastic wrap
- Popsicle sticks
- Paper bowls
- Eggs (or other item to be cooked)

Vocabulary
- Fahrenheit
- Celsius
- Nonrenewable and renewable power
- Incandescent
- Greenhouse gases
- Smog (carbon dioxide)

Purpose

Understanding that solar power is a renewable energy source and can conserve our limited resources is necessary for students to find solutions to today's environmental concerns. Learning about these problems and applying concepts about renewable energy will lead students to adopt the practices needed to secure a clean, environmentally efficient future.

Objectives

Students will gain a better understanding of:
- renewable resources that can replace fossil fuels,
- the history of the oven,
- using and harnessing solar energy,
- converting between Celsius and Fahrenheit,
- the greenhouse effect,
- calculating the volume of a rectangle, and
- finding alternative solutions to environmental issues.

Activity Preparation

1. Run off activity sheets.
2. Gather materials and place them in two different areas of the classroom.
3. Bookmark websites to be used in class.
   a. http://video.nationalgeographic.com/video/environment/energy-environment/solar-power
   b. http://inventors.about.com/od/fstartinventors/ss/Franklin_invent_2.htm
   c. http://www.darvill.clara.net/altenerg/solar.htm
   d. http://vimeo.com/26938601
   e. http://www.pspb.org/e21/media/SolarCooker.html
   f. http://solarcooking.org/sbcdes.htm

Activity Procedure

1. Using an image search, show images of a Dutch oven, and ask students to describe what they are seeing.
2. Show the solar power video (02:39) at Link a., and ask students to summarize the video.
3. Follow up with a question to introduce the topic: "What connection can you make between the oven and the video on solar power?" Inform students that the purpose of today's team challenge is to cook with a solar oven.
4. Distribute activity sheets. Read and discuss information in the first two paragraphs. For an image of the Franklin stove, go to Link b.
5. Teach about Fahrenheit and Celsius. Use the resources you prefer or the information on page 161. Have students practice converting Celsius to Fahrenheit and Fahrenheit to Celsius. Answers to activity sheet: a. 59 degrees C = 138 degrees F; b. 18 degrees C = 64 degrees F; c. –3 degrees F = –19 degrees C; d. 10 degrees F = –12 degrees C.
6. Review the term *renewable resources*. Ask students to brainstorm both nonrenewable resources (oil/gas, natural gas, coal, nuclear) and renewable resources (solar, wind, geothermal, hydro/water).
7. Ask students to list ways we can use solar power (for a detailed list of ideas, go to Link c.). Some ideas for solar power include lights, charging electronics, heating water, cooking, running power, and so on.
8. Ask, "How is solar cooking helping to save lives?" Then show the video on the solar oven (01:02) at Link d. for the answer: Collecting and cooking with firewood is unhealthy, but solar cooking provides a sustainable way to purify water and make it safe to drink. An interesting concept to share with the students is the method used for knowing the temperature

It's Getting Hot in Here

required for this: If it's hot enough to melt wax, it's able to purify the water.

9. Discuss the temperature required to cook an egg. According to experiments, an egg will cook at 103°(although egg distributors recommend 158°). Find out what the current temperature is outdoors, and ask students to discuss ways to increase the temperature of the solar oven. Use the solar cooker simulator at Link e. and the principles of solar cooker design at Link f. for methods to increase the temperature. Ideas to think about include the angle of the sun's rays (slant to face toward the sun); the reflection of light (use reflective material like foil); the use of natural insulators (e.g., cotton, feathers, wood); and the greenhouse effect (use plastic to simulate the greenhouse effect).

10. Introduce the greenhouse effect if students have not brought it up already. The greenhouse effect is the result of heating an enclosed space in which the sun shines through a transparent material, such as glass or plastic. The visible light passes through the glass and is absorbed and reflected by materials within the enclosed space, heating that space.

11. Review the team challenge, answering any questions that students may have.

12. After the challenge has been completed, have students complete their activity sheets.

13. If you wish, assign one of the activities suggested in Extend the Learning With Solar Ovens: Activities.

It's Getting Hot in Here

GOAL

➢ Make a solar oven that cooks an egg the fastest.

MATERIALS

➢ Cardboard
➢ Foil
➢ Plastic wrap

➢ Popsicle sticks
➢ Paper bowls
➢ Eggs (or other item to be cooked)

TIME TO CREATE

➢ 20 minutes

INDIVIDUAL ACTIVITY

Read the following, highlighting important information, and then answer the questions.

Using heat to cook our food is a typical task in most households. We simply turn on an electrical appliance, like a stove or an oven, and prepare the meal. It's easy to take this process and our appliances for granted; however, it took thousands of years to develop the idea of an oven for inside the home.

Since early human existence, people have been using a metal pot over a source of heat for cooking purposes. However, we can thank the Dutch for the development of the oven idea. The concept of the Dutch oven was brought to England and passed on to America in the early 1700s by a man named Abraham Darby. Benjamin Franklin improved upon the Dutch design in 1740 by creating the Pennsylvania fireplace, more commonly known as the Franklin stove. Our current fireplaces are modeled after the design of the Franklin stove.

You may have cooked or eaten food prepared in an outdoor fire pit. Imagine what our life would be like if this was our customary method for cooking. Fast food dining would certainly be a different experience. Your challenge for today will be to use solar energy to cook an egg (or some other edible material) in a solar oven that you and your team will design and create.

German physicist Daniel Gabriel Fahrenheit (1686–1736), inventor of the thermometer, introduced the temperature scale that bears his name: the Fahrenheit scale. Temperature can also be read in terms of Celsius. The Celsius scale, invented by Swedish astronomer Anders Celsius (1701–1744), is also referred to as the "centigrade" scale. Centigrade means "consisting of or divided into 100 degrees." There are 100 Celsius degrees between the freezing point (0 degrees C) and boiling point (100 degrees C) of water. We know that 32 degrees Fahrenheit is equal to 0 degrees Celsius, and the equation to convert Celsius to Fahrenheit is: F = (1.8 x C) + 32. To convert from Fahrenheit to Celsius, subtract 32, and then multiply by 5/9 (or .55). For example, to convert 98.6 degrees Fahrenheit to Celsius: 98.6 – 32 = 66.6; 66.6 (5/9) = 333/9 = 37 degrees Celsius.

Hands-On Engineering © Prufrock Press Inc.

161

Permission is granted to photocopy or reproduce this page for single classroom use only.

1. Calculate the following:

   59° C = _____ F

   18° C = _____ F

2. Calculate the following conversions:

   −3° F = _____ C

   10° F = _____ C

3. Define renewable energy: _____

   _____

   _____

4. Make a list of nonrenewable and renewable power sources.

   Nonrenewable: _____

   _____

   _____

   Renewable: _____

   _____

   _____

5. We recognize the sun's ability to provide energy, referred to as solar power. What are two ways in which we can use solar power? _____

   _____

   _____

6. A solar oven is a really a solar collector; it collects and traps the sun's energy, creating heat. How can we increase the temperature of a solar oven? _____

   _____

   _____

7. What is the greenhouse effect, and how might it help with solar cooking? _____

   _____

   _____

8. Which materials would best help with efficiency in using a solar oven? _____

_____

_____

TEAM CHALLENGE

Participants will work together in teams of two or three for 20 minutes to make a solar oven capable of cooking an egg over time.

When the teacher starts the time, your team will have exactly 20 minutes to gather your materials and build your solar oven. Once the teacher signals that time is up, you must stop working immediately and proceed to the challenge site. Any team that continues to work after the time is up may be disqualified.

Start Time _____ : _____ + 20 Minutes = _____ : _____ End Time

Before the team challenge, complete the following:
1. Sketch your team's oven, and label any additional elements included to increase the heat.

2. Measure the length, width, and height of your oven, and calculate the volume in centimeters.

    Length = _____ cm

    Width = _____ cm

    Height = _____ cm

    Volume = _____ cm

3. What did you use for insulation? _____

4. How did you best utilize the angle of the sun? _____

5. Did you create a greenhouse effect? If so, how? _____

6. What materials did you use to help reflect light? _____

7. What other modifications did you make?_____

8. What is the current temperature? _____

9. How long do you think it will take your team's egg to cook? _____

During the challenge, complete the following:
Record the progress of the egg by describing what the egg looks like at each interval of time. If a thermometer is available, record the temperature at each time interval.

After 5 minutes:_____

Temp =_____

After 10 minutes:_____

Temp =_____

After 15 minutes:_____

Temp =_____

After 20 minutes: _____

Temp =_____

If necessary, use another piece of paper to continue recording the changes until the egg has been cooked.

After the challenge, complete the following:
1. What was the shortest time in which a team was able to cook its egg? _____

2. What might have helped (besides using electricity) your team's egg cook in less time? ____

   _____

   _____

3. Summarize your information on the progress, from beginning to end, of cooking an egg in your solar oven. _____

   _____

   _____

4. Would you be able to adapt to a living environment where the only source of power was through the sun, wind, and water? Explain why or why not. _____

   _____

   _____

EXTEND THE LEARNING WITH SOLAR OVENS: ACTIVITIES

1. **Investigate fluorescent versus incandescent light bulbs.** Incandescent means emitting light as a result of being heated. Incandescent light bulbs contain a filament that glows white-hot when heated by a current that is passed through. If every U.S. household replaced just one incandescent light bulb with a fluorescent light bulb, it would save a vast amount of resources. View a short video (01:45) on light bulbs at http://www.vimeo.com/26932156, and do further research. Think of a product that will help you share this information—a speech, a blog, a video, and so on. Be creative! Share your product with your classmates.

2. **Build a solar water heater.** Investigate how water is heated in a solar water heater. You will need the following materials:
   - a clear plastic 1-gallon container,
   - a 4-oz jar with two holes drilled in the lid,
   - two pieces of drinking straws glued in the holes so they stick out 1/4" above and below the lid, and
   - food coloring.

   Process:
   - Fill the 1-gallon container with cold water.
   - Fill the 4-oz jar with hot water, add food coloring to the hot water, put the lid on, and place the 4-oz jar inside the 1-gallon container.
   - Because the colored water is hotter, and hot molecules take up more space than cold molecules do, the colored water will rise up through the straw to the top of the cold water in the 1-gallon container.

   Citing your experiment, write a couple of paragraphs about how hot water is heated in a solar water heater.

3. **Do a cool solar car project.** Working with a team of classmates or with your whole class, go to http://www.nrel.gov/docs/gen/fy01/30828.pdf. This solar car lesson will take you through a detailed process of designing and building a solar car. Along the way, you will learn about engineering components of aerodynamics, as well as car parts (chassis, transmission, body shell, wheel and bearings, and motor).

The Amazing Trampoline Act

Make a trampoline that will provide an object with the highest rebound.

Subjects and Skills
- ◆ Physical science
- ◆ Kinetic energy, potential energy, friction
- ◆ The history of trampolines (recreational, in wars)

Materials
- ◆ Fabric scraps
- ◆ Sheets of plastic
- ◆ String or yarn
- ◆ Coffee containers
- ◆ Rubber bands
- ◆ Shoe boxes
- ◆ Paper clips
- ◆ Golf balls or marbles

Vocabulary
- ◆ Tether
- ◆ Trampoline
- ◆ Rebound
- ◆ Kinetic energy
- ◆ Potential energy
- ◆ Bounce
- ◆ Friction

Purpose

Understanding how bounce is created and how physics affects rebound is important in engineering. Students will apply kinetic and potential energy and Newton's laws of gravitation to their trampoline designs.

Objectives

Students will gain a better understanding of:
- ◆ the history of the trampoline,
- ◆ kinetic and potential energy,
- ◆ friction,
- ◆ creating rebound,
- ◆ finding measurements to the nearest 1/8 of an inch, and

♦ applying the equation E = KE + PE (total energy = kinetic energy + potential energy).

Activity Preparation

1. Run off activity sheets.
2. Gather materials and place them in two different areas of the room.
3. Bookmark websites to be used in class.
   a. http://www.funny-games.biz/trampoline.html
   b. http://www.cbc.ca/kids/games/trampoline
   c. http://scratch.mit.edu/projects/goalkeepery/1519921
   d. http://scratch.mit.edu/projects/dapontes/843278

Activity Procedure

1. Start off the lesson by asking, "What do Eskimos (Inuit-Yupiks), fire fighters, and circus performers have in common?" After students guess, say that they all use a form of trampolines either for recreation or for their careers. Ask if students have ever jumped on a trampoline. After discussion, distribute the activity sheet. To further discussion, ask how Eskimos might have used trampolines. (Eskimos would use a walrus skin to play with their children. They would throw the child up into the air and then catch them with the walrus skin.) Ask how fire fighters use trampolines (to help people jump out of burning buildings).
2. Continue reading the history of trampolines. Discuss ways trampolines have been used in the military: They helped train aerial awareness through providing aerial orientation, reduced fears of falling, gave practice being upside down and revolving in midair, developed balance and body control while being in midair, and provided mental and physical conditioning (e.g., cardiovascular endurance, muscle tension in arms, legs, and abdominals).
3. Discuss the concept of rebound. Rebound means to spring or move back.
4. There are several interactive trampoline games to demonstrate bounce. Go to Link a., Link b., and/or Link c.
5. Review kinetic and potential energy. (Kinetic energy is the movement of an object. Potential energy is energy stored in an object.) With the trampoline example, potential energy is the energy in the stretched springs; kinetic energy is the action of the net and/or the object on the net.
6. Ask students to explain bounce (a change in direction of motion after hitting an obstacle) and friction.
7. Review the answers for Question 9. When a ball is held up in the air it has **potential** energy but no **kinetic** energy. When it is let go, it starts falling because of **gravity**, and as it falls its **potential** energy is reduced, while its

kinetic energy increases. After it hits the ground, the ball should bounce back a little lower than the height at which it was dropped. So after the first bounce, it has less potential energy than it did originally because of **friction**. When the ball bounces, it changes shape slightly. The compression and change in shape is friction that converts some of the kinetic energy in the form of heat, or thermal energy.

8. Help students understand E = KE + PE (total energy = kinetic energy + potential energy) with the interactive at Link d.

9. Review the team challenge, answering any questions that students may have. Hold the challenge in whatever manner is easiest and most appropriate for your classroom.

10. Once the challenge has been completed, allow students to finish their activity sheets.

11. If you wish, use Extend the Learning With Trampolines: Teacher Guide to help you guide the students to create their own trampoline computer games.

The Amazing Trampoline Act

GOAL

➤ Make a trampoline that will provide an object with the highest rebound.

MATERIALS

➤ Fabric scraps
➤ Sheets of plastic
➤ String or yarn
➤ Coffee containers
➤ Rubber bands
➤ Shoe boxes
➤ Paper clips
➤ Golf balls or marbles

TIME TO CREATE

➤ 20 minutes

INDIVIDUAL ACTIVITY

Read the following, highlighting important information, and then answer the questions.

What do Eskimos (Inuit Yupiks), fire fighters, and circus performers have in common? They all use a form of trampolines for either recreation or their careers.

The actual creation of the trampoline in its modern form is credited to two men: George Nissen and Larry Griswold. Around 1935, Griswold, an assistant gymnastics coach at The University of Iowa, and Nissen, a tumbler on The University of Iowa gymnastics team, developed the idea of a "bouncing rig" from observing trapeze performers practice with tumbler nets. The men altered the tumbler net by attaching a large piece of stretched canvas to an iron frame, using coil springs as a tether, and created the "bouncing rig." On a trip to Mexico, Nissen heard the word *trampolin*, which means diving board in Spanish. Nissen liked the sound of it and decided to change the spelling and call his new bouncing rig a trampoline. In addition to being used by fire fighters, gymnasts, and circus performers, during World War II, trampolines proved to be an integral part of military training for both pilots and naval cadets.

Do you remember why Sir Isaac Newton is famous? If you think it's because he discovered the law of gravity, you're partially correct. Newton did not actually discover gravity; he merely defined it mathematically. Newton's Law of Universal Gravitation explains that the greater an object's mass, the greater its gravitational force.

1. What is the purpose of a tumbler net? _____
2. How might trampolines have helped with training pilots during World War II? _____

_____

_____

Hands-On Engineering © Prufrock Press Inc.

Permission is granted to photocopy or reproduce this page for single classroom use only.

169

3. Define rebound. _____

4. How would you measure the rebound of an object such as a golf ball? _____

    _____

    _____

5. Approximately how long would it take for a.) a feather dropped from your school's roof to reach the ground?_____ b.) a rock dropped from your school's roof to reach the ground? _____ What is the difference in your estimations? Explain why there might be a difference in the amount of time for these items to reach the ground. _____

    _____

    _____

6. Kinetic and potential energy are related to Newton's ideas. Briefly explain the energies below.

    Kinetic: _____

    Potential: _____

7. Explain kinetic and potential energies using a trampoline as an example. _____

    _____

    _____

8. What is bounce?_____

    _____

9. When a ball is dropped and hits the floor, it stops. At this point, the molecules of the ball will be compressed in some places and stretched apart in others; this is an example of friction. Friction is the force that creates resistance when coming into contact with a moving object. Complete the following sentences: When a ball is held up in the air it has _____ energy but no _____ energy. When it is let go, it starts falling because of _____, and as it falls its _____ energy is reduced, while its _____ energy increases. After it hits the ground, the ball should bounce back a little lower than the height at which it was dropped. So after the first bounce, it has less potential energy than it did originally. Why? _____

10. The equation E = KE + PE (total energy = kinetic energy + potential energy) can be used to find the energy of the jump. In the jump, kinetic energy decreases due to the velocity of the jump, and potential energy increases. Therefore, the greater the speed and force of the jump, the larger the jump will be. Think about how the design of a trampoline could cause the greatest rebound of an object. List the elements that are important for this to occur: _____

    _____

    _____

TEAM CHALLENGE

Participants will work together in teams of two or three for 20 minutes to make a trampoline that provides the highest rebound of a golf ball or a marble. Each team will have three tries.

When the teacher starts the time, your team will have exactly 20 minutes to gather your supplies and build your trampoline. When the teacher signals that the time is up, stop working immediately and take your trampoline to the test site. Any team that continues to work after time has been called may be disqualified.

Start Time _____ : _____ + 20 Minutes = _____ : _____ End Time

Record measurements to the nearest 1/8 inch of the height of the rebound.

Trial 1: _____ inches

Trial 2: _____ inches

Trial 3: _____ inches

After the challenge, complete the following questions:

1. What materials did your team use that would provide the best advantage? _____

2. What was the difference between the highest and the lowest rebounds for your team? _____

3. Record the class's lowest rebound. _____

4. Record the class's highest rebound. _____

5. What was the difference between the class's lowest and highest rebounds? _____

6. What makes a trampoline provide a better rebound? _____

7. What design modifications could be made to make a better trampoline? _____

8. How might trampolines and/or the principles of trampolines help us in the future? _____

EXTEND THE LEARNING WITH TRAMPOLINES: TEACHER'S GUIDE

Guide students in designing a bouncing ball or pong game. Visit http://scratch.mit.edu. Designed with learning and education in mind by the Massachusetts Institute of Technology, Scratch is a free program that makes it easy to create interactive stories, animation, games, music, and art. Students will develop important design and problem-solving skills, apply creative thinking, reason systematically, and work collaboratively.

A teacher's forum is available at http://scratched.media.mit.edu/discussions/new-forum for collaboration, teaching strategies, and information. Even if you don't consider yourself a techie, your students will definitely benefit from learning their way around the techie world. The trampoline lesson is a great segue into the technical arena. Tell students they will be navigating this site in order to create their own games involving the concepts they have learned in this lesson, keeping it fairly open ended.

It's best to schedule the time in a computer lab and allow the students to navigate the site and figure it out largely on their own. You do not actually need to know how to use the site—you only need to facilitate. Print the information at http://www.smm.org/ltc/files/simplegame.pdf to guide students along this extension project.

Zip-a-Dee-Doo-Dah

Make a zip line that will carry an object a specific distance (about 10 ft across) and be able to stop at a specific location without damaging or dropping the object. Every team that accomplishes this challenge will be declared victorious!

Subjects and Skills

- Measurement conversion
- Calculating distance, speed, and time
- Potential and kinetic energy, gravity, friction

Materials

- String
- Paper clips
- Cardboard tubing
- Paper cups
- Index cards
- Metersticks/yardsticks
- Areas where students can anchor and operate zip lines

Vocabulary

- Potential energy
- Kinetic energy
- Acceleration

Purpose

Understanding how to apply scientific concepts of motion and forces is important to the fundamental engineering and design principles. Students will use mathematical skills with algebraic equations, problem solving, and conversion of units as they design and create zip lines. The physical elements of potential and kinetic energy will be applied with the design of the function of the zip line.

Objectives

Students will gain a better understanding of:
- the applications of transferring energy,

Zip-a-Dee-Doo-Dah

- principles of potential and kinetic energy,
- Newton's Law of Universal Gravitation and how it affects acceleration of an object,
- applying the Distance = Speed x Time equation,
- converting units, and
- applying concepts of friction to serve a purpose for the design.

Activity Preparation

1. Run off activity sheets.
2. Gather materials and place them in two different areas of the room.
3. Bookmark websites to be used in class.
   a. http://vimeo.com/27164844
   b. http://vimeo.com/27163861

Activity Procedure

1. Distribute the activity sheet, and read and discuss it with students.
2. Ask students to respond to Question 1, without giving them the answers (delivering supplies to remote areas, transportation in and out of areas, dropping object on target).
3. Show the video (03:44) at Link a. of children relying on zip line.
4. Introduce the term velocity (speed). Ask students to explain ways we measure velocity (e.g., speedometer, radar). Continue by introducing the formula Distance = Velocity (or Speed) x Time; also Speed = Distance/Time. Answers: 2.) 45 = 9 x 5; 3.) Speed = Distance / Time; 4.) 30 mph; 5.) Division, 15 miles; 6.) 4 hours; 7.) 1800 ft/min.).
5. Show the video (02:08) at Link b. for students to practice finding velocity. Answer to Question 8: The zip line takes 54 seconds. To solve how many feet per minute, distance (5,330) = 54 x Speed; Speed = 98.7 ft/sec. (5,922 ft/min). Extend the thinking to solve for yards per minute (1,974), miles per minute (1.12), and miles per hour (67.2).
6. Continue with the lesson by discussing how the height of a line affects the speed of an object. Answers: 9.) The steeper the line, the faster the speed; 10.) 2 ft/sec; 120 ft/min; 7,200 ft/hour; approximately 1.4 mi/hr.
7. Review how friction can be used to oppose the force of gravity. Friction is needed to maintain a slower, desired speed. Friction will also be necessary for the object to stop the object's movement in a controlled manner.
8. Review the team challenge, answering any questions students may have. Assign teams and team numbers.
9. After the challenge is completed, have students complete the activity sheets.
10. If you wish, assign one of the activities suggested in Extend the Learning With Zip Lines: Activities.

Zip-a-Dee-Doo-Dah

GOAL

> ➤ Make a zip line that will carry an object a specific distance (about 10 ft across) and be able to stop at a specific location without damaging or dropping the object. Every team that accomplishes this challenge will be declared victorious!

MATERIALS

> ➤ String
> ➤ Paper clips
> ➤ Cardboard tubing

> ➤ Paper cups
> ➤ Index cards
> ➤ Metersticks or yardsticks

TIME TO CREATE

> ➤ 20 minutes

INDIVIDUAL ACTIVITY

Read and respond to the following questions:

1. Author H. G. Wells (1866–1946) wrote many novels that are classics in the science fiction genre, such as *War of the Worlds*, *The Time Machine*, and *The Island of Dr. Moreau*. In his novel *The Invisible Man*, written in 1897, Wells introduces his readers to the concept of a zip line. Today's zip lines are generally used for recreational purposes; however, zip lines also provide useful services. Name one way in which zip lines can be used to assist others.

   _____

   _____

2. When we talk about speed, we often use words like "really fast" or "kind of slow," but many times we need to be able to measure the actual speed of a moving object. If you know the distance the object travels and how long it takes to get there (time), you can calculate the actual speed of an object. Read the following and figure out the formula for measuring the speed of an object. Traveling at a speed of 9 miles per hour, it took John 5 hours to ride his bicycle 45 miles.

   First write the problem as an equation:

   _____ = _____ ___ _____

3. There is a mathematical equation that works for calculating the speed of an object. The equation to calculate speed of an object is: _____

4. Try your equation out on finding the speed of the boat.

   Speed of boat = _____ mph, Distance of travel = 60 miles, Time = 2 hours

5. What is the opposite of multiplication? _____ Change the order of the formula in order to calculate the distance Henry traveled given the speed and time. Traveling at 5 miles per hour in 3 hours, Henry walked a distance of _____ miles.

6. Calculate the time the dog traveled with information providing the speed and distance: How long did it take the dog to travel 48 miles if he went at a speed of 12 mph? _____

_____

7. Not all calculations will have the same units of hours to hours and minutes to minutes. For example, a baseball would not typically travel for an hour. If you know the speed in hours, but the object travels for less than a minute, you would need to convert the units. Hours might need to be converted to minutes, minutes might need to be converted to seconds, and so on. For example, if a baseball traveled 90 feet in 3 seconds, how many feet would it have traveled in 1 minute? Notice the units. Because 60 seconds = 1 minute, figure out the speed in seconds per minute, then convert to how fast the ball would travel in 1 minute. Speed of the ball = _____ ft/min, Distance of travel = 90 ft, Time = 3 seconds.

8. For today's team challenge, you will design and create a zip line. You will also calculate the speed of an object traveling on a zip line. Use the video that you watch as a class for practice.

   Calculate the speed of the zip line in the video: _____

   Convert to feet per minute: _____

9. How does the height of one side of the line affect the speed of the object?_____

   _____

   _____

10. Calculate the velocity of a spool of thread traveling along an angled string:
    Distance = 10 ft, Time = 5 sec; Speed = _____ ft/sec
    _____ ft/min
    _____ ft/hr
    _____ mi/hr

11. Conserving energy is helpful when engineering a zip line. At the top of the line, you can use gravitational potential energy, and at the bottom, friction can help to transform the gravitational potential energy to kinetic energy. To allow for maintaining a desired speed, most zip lines level off a bit after the initial drop. Once you reach the desired speed, the angle needs to match the force of friction. When this happens, you will maintain your current speed.

    How will you include a source of friction in your zip line? _____

    _____

    _____

TEAM CHALLENGE

Participants will work together in teams of two or three for 20 minutes to make a 10-ft zip line that will carry an object and stop at a given point without dropping or damaging the object. Every team that accomplishes this challenge will be declared victorious!

When the teacher starts the time, your team will have exactly 20 minutes to gather your materials and build your zip line. Once your teacher signals that time is up, you must stop working immediately. Any team that continues to work after time has been called may be disqualified.

Start Time _____ : _____ + 20 Minutes = _____ : _____ End Time

Experiment with the height until you find the lowest height that would enable the object to travel smoothly all the way to the end. Measure this height, calculate the speed, and record it in the chart. Remember: Speed = Distance/Time. Experiment with the height until you find the one that enables you to best achieve your goal. You may only use one height for your zip line in the class challenge.

Lowest Height of String:	Hightest Height of String:
Speed:	Speed:
Distance:	Distance:
Time:	Time:

After the team challenge, complete the following questions:

1. What was your team's object's fastest time?_____

   What was the height for this time?_____

2. What was the lowest height for your team's zip line?_____

   What was the time for this height?_____

3. Write a brief summary of the relationship between height, time, and speed.

   _____

   _____

4. Consider the following information:
   - Newton's First Law states that as an object travels down the zip line, it builds forward speed. It will continue at that speed until a force acts on it, such as hitting the stopping points.
   - Acceleration means that an object's speed increases as it falls due to Earth's gravitational pull.
   - The object's stored (potential) energy changes to motion (kinetic) energy as it falls.

In thinking about this information, how could you improve your team's zip line?

_____

_____

_____

_____

_____

_____

EXTEND THE LEARNING WITH ZIP LINES: ACTIVITIES

1. **Use the Pythagorean theorem.** Work in groups of three or four with classmates to apply your knowledge of the Pythagorean theorem to make a zip line for a playground. Test three different slopes of the zip line to investigate the relationship of the slope of the line to the time it takes an object to slide down the line. Choose the most appropriate measure of central tendency (mean, median, or mode) to reflect your data, graph your data, and create an analysis of materials and expenses in order to complete the construction of the zip line.

   Follow these steps:
   - Complete a scaled drawing of the zip line.
   - Begin with an initial height (50 cm) to start the trials.
   - Record all information on a grid, with the horizontal labels including the following: Initial Height (height of triangle), Length of String (creating the hypotenuse), Measurement From the Wall (base of triangle), Time in Seconds (Trial 1, Trial 2, and Trial 3), and Measure of Central Tendency.
   - Use the Pythagorean theorem to calculate the theoretical distance for the length of the string.
   - Graph the coordinate points (height, slope) to show the relationship.

2. **Batter up!** Research famous baseball pitchers to find the fastest pitch in miles per hour in recorded baseball history. Use this information to calculate the speed of this pitch per minute and per hour. Consider this problem:

   One of the fastest pitches recorded was Nolan Ryan's 100.9 mph on August 20, 1974. The distance between home plate and the pitcher's mound is 60 ft, 6 in. (18.39 m). How long did it take the baseball to travel from the mound to the plate? _____

   How far would the baseball travel in 1 hour? _____

   Write and solve a set of your own factual baseball pitch velocity problems based on your research.

3. **The zip-lining ping-pong ball.** Build a zip line that will take a ping-pong ball 4 seconds to travel from the top to the bottom. Go to the PBS Design Squad Nation (http://pbskids.org/designsquad/video/index.html) and click on the DIY Zip Line video in the right scroll bar for a demonstration.

Breaking Down Barriers

Construct a battering ram capable of knocking over other teams' walls. Construct a wall to withstand the forces of other teams' battering rams.

Subjects and Skills

- The history of battering rams, castles, and walls
- Geometry

Materials

- String
- Spools
- Straws
- Three unsharpened pencils per team
- Paper cups
- Paper plates
- Egg cartons

Vocabulary

- Battering ram

Purpose

Students will learn and apply the structural concepts associated with castle design. These concepts will enhance their understanding of structural integrity, the utilization of simple machines, and how gravity can be used to generate force.

Objectives

Students will gain a better understanding of:
- the various modes of protection incorporated in castles' designs,
- military inventions and the design and purpose of the battering ram,
- how simple machines (wheels) can be used to solve design problems, and
- how gravity can be used to generate force.

Activity Preparation

1. Run off activity sheets.
2. Gather materials and place them in two separate areas of the room.

3. Bookmark websites to be used in class.
   a. http://www.youtube.com/watch?v=o_w4FGgOVsM
   b. http://www.castles.me.uk/battering-ram.htm
   c. http://science.discovery.com/videos/what-the-ancients-knew-the-battering-ram.html
   d. https://vimeo.com/38339356

Activity Procedure

1. Show the video (02:54) on medieval castle design at Link a.
2. Ask students to discuss the various modes of protection included in the design of the castle. (They might mention the tall outer wall, the moat, high towers for surveillance, built-in bows and places to fire arrows, arrow slits and notches, a drawbridge, heavy wooden doors protected by a thick metal grate, murder holes in which to dump oil and large rocks on enemies, and enclosed courtyards.)
3. Ask students to brainstorm ways to get through the walled barriers. Lead the responses toward a method to weaken the walls (e.g., a battering ram, a trebuchet, or some other wall-breaking method). For more information on the battering ram, go to Link b.
4. Distribute the activity sheets. Students will read information and respond to Question 1.
5. Discuss information and students' responses (e.g., add wheels, put it on a cart). Show the video (00:36) at Link c. This battering ram was used for naval warfare against the Greeks; however, the concept is the same as the one used in land versions.
6. While students are sketching their rams, select teams for the team challenge, and assign team numbers.
7. Students will continue through Question 3. Show the video (00:16) on castle stonework at Link d. Explain that cement has been around since ancient Macedonia.
8. Ask students to think about how skyscrapers were engineered to withstand the elements of wind, rain, and earthquakes. Using these ideas, ask students to respond to Question 4. Answers might include adding wire to the bricks, doubling the bricks, using stronger adhesive, and so on.
9. Explain that the team challenge will include two parts: making a battering ram and building a wall able to resist another team's battering ram. Discuss the materials available for building both the wall and the ram.
10. While students are designing their rams and walls, decide which teams will battle each other (create a bracket). Teams will alternate turns using their rams against the other teams' walls. Each team will have only five tries to destroy the other team's wall. Remind students that they will not

Breaking Down Barriers

be able to touch the other team's wall with anything other than the swing of the timber piece of the battering ram. The goal is to destroy the opponent's wall in five tries or fewer. Teams will keep track of the result of each attempt. You may allow teams to rebuild their walls to learn from design mistakes, if you wish. If there is enough time, you may decide to continue rounds for victorious teams to compete against other victorious teams until one wall remains standing.

11. Review the team challenge, answering any questions students may have, and assign teams (of four or five students each) and team numbers.

12. Once the challenge is over, have students complete the activity sheets.

13. If you wish, use Extend the Learning With Medieval Construction: Google SketchUp Project to guide students in designing their own castles.

Breaking Down Barriers

GOAL

➢ Construct a battering ram capable of knocking over other teams' walls. Construct a wall to withstand the forces of other teams' battering rams.

MATERIALS

➢ String
➢ Spools
➢ Straws
➢ Three unsharpened pencils per team

➢ Paper cups
➢ Paper plates
➢ Egg cartons

TIME TO CREATE

➢ 20 minutes

INDIVIDUAL ACTIVITY

Read the following, highlighting important information, and then answer the questions.

One of the earliest sophisticated military inventions was the battering ram. Military engineers in 2500 B.C. designed the battering ram to batter, pummel, pound, and basically destroy the walls and gatehouse doors of medieval castles.

The battering ram consisted of a long, heavy beam of timber with a tapered trunk. Its point was capped with iron, which made it look similar to the head of a ram. Due to its weight, the battering ram needed a way to be transported to various sites.

Soldiers swung the trunk of the battering ram back and forth; the forward end of the trunk moved in and out like a tortoise's head, battering its target. Battering rams enabled armies to pry stones loose from walls in order to weaken the structure and tear it down. Castle defenders would try to burn the battering ram down with flaming arrows; however, a blanket made of animal pelts or mud was able to protect the battering ram against the flames.

1. How might battering rams have been designed in order to be mobile?

    _____

    _____

2. On the next page, sketch a battering ram using the description above. Include the means for transportation and protection.

Hands-On Engineering © Prufrock Press Inc.

183

Permission is granted to photocopy or reproduce this page for single classroom use only.

```



```

3. How were builders able to create castle walls in which the stones stayed in place? _____

   _____

   _____

4. Thinking like an engineer, how would you build a wall today strong enough to resist a battering ram? _____

   _____

   _____

TEAM ACTIVITY

   Participants will work together in teams of four or five for 20 minutes to make a battering ram that is able to knock down another team's wall and to build a wall capable of resisting another team's battering ram.

   Your team will be paired with another team, and each team will have five opportunities to try to knock down the other team's wall with its battering ram using **only** the gravity of the swing of the timber piece of the battering ram. Members may not push or manipulate other components of the structure. No team member may touch the opponents' or their own wall at any point during the competition. Failure to follow these rules will automatically result in victory for the opposing team.

   When the teacher starts the time, your team will have exactly 20 minutes to gather your materials and build your battering ram and wall. Once the teacher signals that time is up, stop working immediately and proceed to the challenge site. Any team that continues to work after time is up may be disqualified.

   Start Time _____ : _____ + 20 Minutes = _____ : _____ End Time

Before the challenge, complete the following items:

1. Draw a sketch of what your team's battering ram will look like (using the available materials).

2. What materials will your team use for the wall? _____

    _____

    _____

3. Decide which members will make the battering ram and which will build the wall.

    Ram: _____

    Wall: _____

During the challenge, complete the following chart (the results of each attempt must be completed):

Was the wall unscathed, weakened, or destroyed in each attempt?

Attempt 1

Your team's wall: _____

Opponent's wall: _____

Attempt 2

Your team's wall: _____

Opponent's wall: _____

Attempt 3

Your team's wall: _____

Opponent's wall: _____

Attempt 4

Your team's wall: _____

Opponent's wall: _____

Attempt 5

Your team's wall: _____

Opponent's wall: _____

After the challenge, complete the following questions:

1. Summarize the results of what took place during this event. What did you notice? What contributed to the results? _____

   _____

   _____

2. How would you modify your team's wall to provide more stability? _____

   _____

   _____

3. How would you modify your team's battering ram to generate more power? _____

   _____

   _____

EXTEND THE LEARNING WITH MEDIEVAL CONSTRUCTION: GOOGLE SKETCHUP PROJECT

Build a castle. Google SketchUp enables you to create 3D models of everything from simple geometric forms to complex communities. You will design a virtual medieval castle scene complete with towers, defensive walls, inside buildings, and so on. The scene will include people, trees, and weapons as seen during medieval times. For an example, go to http://sketchup.google.com/3dwarehouse/details?mid=bf531fd815ae2bbeb6befb2adbdfbfb5.

Follow these directions to get started:

- Download and install the Google SketchUp Viewer from http://sketchup.google.com. The Google application will prompt you through the installation process. This is a one-time setup that installs the Google SketchUp Viewer to enable you to view Google 3D SketchUp models.
- Go to https://support.google.com/sketchup/bin/answer.py?hl=en&answer=95079&topic=1700331&rd=1 and select detailed instructions and information for either Mac or PC users.
- Examples of castles available to download are available at http://sketchup.google.com/3dwarehouse/cldetails?clid=71f153d8dd5b41e8897467e55536c415&scoring=r.
- The Google 3D Warehouse (http://sketchup.google.com/3dwh/) is a free, online repository where you can find, share, store, and collaborate on 3D models.

Your model must look realistic and be modeled to scale. Include a variety of 3D shapes: rectangular and circular towers, walkways, and arch-shaped openings. Include human figures, trees, and appropriate weapons (these may be downloaded).

World's Fair

Construct a design that serves a particular purpose or addresses a specific problem in society.

Subjects and Skills

- Science, innovation, identifying problems and opportunities
- Math, adapting concepts to design needs

Materials

- Any materials remaining in the classroom collection

Vocabulary

- Biosphere

Purpose

Students will have the opportunity to apply engineering concepts to real-life problems by creating their own hands-on designs. Wherever people exist, issues and concerns associated with design and engineering will be present. Teaching students engineering and design concepts is important; however, teaching them how to apply the skills they have learned to future situations is what will ensure their success.

Objectives

Students will:
- research current environmental concerns and issues,
- select a specific topic and explore further associated problems,
- think about possible solutions,
- design a plan to address the problems, and
- create a presentation to teach others about their issue and design.

Activity Preparation

1. Run off activity sheets.
2. Gather materials (all of the leftover materials from other challenges, at your discretion) and place them in two different areas of the room.

3. Bookmark websites to be used in class. (Include additional sites that are newsworthy or current, along with any you think may be of particular interest to your students.)

   a. http://pbskids.org/designsquad/projects/index.html

Activity Procedure

1. Ask students to summarize what they have learned from these design and engineering challenges. Explain that their final challenge will be to create their own designs.

2. Discuss advances in science, technology, and engineering, using any websites you have bookmarked.

3. Distribute the activity sheets, and allow time for students to read and respond to Question 1.

4. Discuss what future engineers may need to design (e.g., more advanced prosthetic limbs), as well as novelty inventions (e.g., a device to peel a banana). Encourage students to think outside the box. Ask students to discuss new technology that has developed over the past 5 years. Ask students think about ways in which people can use new technologies and engineering concepts and skills to help the world.

5. Continue the lesson through a class discussion about past ideas and potential designs. Visit the site at Link a. to foster ideas. As students are completing their activity sheets, organize the materials to be used in the challenge, if you have not already done so.

6. Read and review the challenge, and answer any questions that students may have. You will decide whether students work individually or in teams. Students (or teams) will have some time to brainstorm and sketch their designs, and then the timed design and building portion will begin.

7. You could extend this lesson by making it more of a research project to allow individual students or teams to gather information.

8. If you wish, use Extend the Learning With Independent Design: Teaching Suggestions to have students explore additional independent design opportunities.

World's Fair

Name: _____ Date: _____

World's Fair

GOAL

➢ Construct a design that serves a particular purpose or addresses a specific problem in society.

MATERIALS

➢ Materials remaining in the classroom collection

TIME TO CREATE

➢ 30 minutes

INDIVIDUAL ACTIVITY

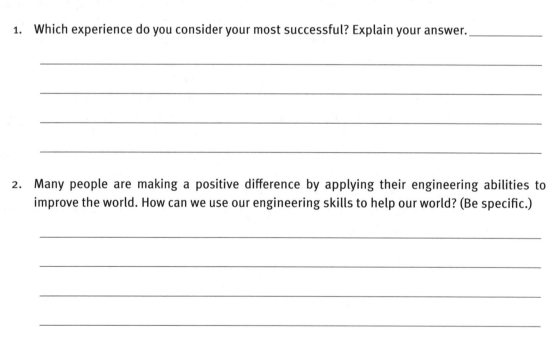

You have been presented with a variety of design challenges in which you were required to work with limited resources. It is now time to test what you have learned. Think about the various designs you have created, the results of the activities, and some unique uses for materials. Take into account the cause and effect of some of the events in which you have participated.

1. Which experience do you consider your most successful? Explain your answer. _____

   _____

   _____

   _____

   _____

2. Many people are making a positive difference by applying their engineering abilities to improve the world. How can we use our engineering skills to help our world? (Be specific.)

   _____

   _____

   _____

   _____

Hands-On Engineering © Prufrock Press Inc.

3. This is your ultimate challenge: Construct a unique design, different from any you have completed during this past year, that serves a particular purpose in society. List the materials that are available to you:_____

_____

_____

_____

_____

4. Designing and engineering require the ability to think beyond the present. You have learned about a couple of Leonardo da Vinci's ideas (parachute and helicopter). Some of his ideas came to fruition 500 years after he first thought of them. In today's world, we need to be like da Vinci and think ahead of our time. What concerns do we have in today's world and society that must be addressed? _____

_____

_____

_____

_____

5. As you reflect on each of the potential designs below, write notes in the margins to contribute during the class discussion. Think about modern challenges, big and small, and potential issues and solutions.

Here are a few examples of inventions developed by students in other classes:
   ➢ A tool with which to measure pollution
   ➢ A machine to safely prevent animals from stealing food from bird feeders
   ➢ A portable tool with which to purify water
   ➢ A tree house in an area without many trees
   ➢ An umbrella that hovers above without needing to be held
   ➢ A method to pour standard amounts of cereal and milk into a bowl

6. Brainstorm two or three designs of your own and their purpose. Record them here.

   a. _____

   _____

   b. _____

   _____

   c. _____

   _____

TEAM CHALLENGE

The teacher will decide how groups will be selected or if you will work individually. When the teacher announces the start time, you will have 30 minutes to get your supplies and make your design challenge. Your goal is to make a useful and creative design.

If you are working in a team, share ideas with other members. Discuss purposes and possibilities of designs. Decide which design your team will create, and be cooperative, because time is limited. Work on the following questions individually, and when prompted, discuss them with your team members.

1. Describe the design you will make. _____
    _____
    _____

2. What is the function of this design? _____
    _____

3. How many moving parts does it have? _____
4. How are the moving parts connected to each other? _____
    _____
    _____

5. What does each moving part do in the design?_____
    _____
    _____

6. Make a list of materials you think will be needed. _____
    _____
    _____

7. Sketch a diagram of your design. Add arrows and written notes to indicate directions of motion for each part, label the elements of the machines involved, and explain any other connections.

8. If you are working with other students, compare your sketch with the sketches of your teammates. How are the sketches alike and different?

_____

_____

Once all teams have had sufficient brainstorming and planning time, your teacher will begin the timer. You will have 30 minutes to gather your materials and build your design. Your goal is to make a useful and creative design and explain how the design helps to address some purpose, problem, or issue. Once time is up, you must stop working immediately and proceed to the challenge site to present your design. Any team that continues to work after time is up may be disqualified from the contest.

Start Time _____ : _____ + 30 Minutes = _____ : _____ End Time

Before the challenge, write brief notes to prepare for your design presentation.

_____

_____

_____

_____

_____

_____

_____

_____

_____

_____

The class will provide appropriate feedback on your design. Take notes about what sort of feedback you receive (i.e., praise, criticisms, questions, suggestions).

_____

_____

_____

_____

_____

_____

_____

_____

_____

_____

_____

_____

_____

_____

_____

_____

_____

_____

_____

_____

_____

_____

_____

Make a final analysis of your design. How could it be improved? What are its strong points?

_____

_____

_____

_____

_____

_____

_____

_____

_____

_____

_____

_____

_____

_____

_____

_____

_____

_____

_____

_____

EXTEND THE LEARNING WITH INDEPENDENT DESIGN: TEACHING SUGGESTIONS

We teach because we value kids and our future, and we invest our time in making a difference in our world—exponentially. Teaching students about design and engineering principles through a process that allows kids to explore, question, create, analyze, redesign, and engage in their own learning will prepare them to think. Our students will someday be living in an environment that includes technology we can only imagine. Along with this new technology, new problems and possibilities will emerge. Through the activities in this book, students have learned to apply mathematical, scientific, and logical thinking when faced with solving problems.

Engineering design projects will inspire students to want to embrace math and science as tools. The more they learn about math and science, the better their engineering and design abilities will become. The following activities and resources will continue to foster students' curiosity through design and engineering.

1. **NASA's future flight design.** Visit http://futureflight.arc.nasa.gov to let students become NASA researchers and incorporate engineering principles in the design of an improved air transportation system of the future.
2. **Make electricity with water.** Visit http://www.ehow.com/how_4759562_make-electricity-water.html to access a lesson created by Isaiah David, freelance writer and musician, on making electricity with water. Students will learn about hydroelectric energy and develop a better understanding of the potential for utilizing natural resources.
3. **Make water rockets.** Visit http://exploration.grc.nasa.gov/education/rocket/BottleRocket/about.htm to show students how to turn plastic soda pop bottles into water rockets as they learn about propulsion.
4. **Design a habitable planet.** Visit http://astroventure.arc.nasa.gov to have students participate in an "astroventure" as they travel to the future and think like NASA designers/engineers. Students can collaborate with other scientists as they search and build a habitable planet.
5. **Independent building.** Visit http://www.build-it-yourself.com, where students can team up with Invention Universe. Build It Yourself is an outstanding resource site for students to continue exploring engineering and designing ideas in multiple directions.

References

International Society for Technology in Education. (2008). *National education technology standards for students.* Retrieved from http://www.iste.org/Libraries/PDFs/NETS-T_Standards.sflb.ashx

International Technology Education Association. (2007). *Standards for technological literacy* (3rd ed.). Retrieved from http://www.iteaconnect.org/TAA/PDFs/xstnd.pdf

National Council of Teachers of Mathematics. (2000). *Principles and standards for school mathematics* (3rd ed.). Reston, VA: Author.

National Governors Association. (2007). *Building a science, technology, engineering and math agenda.* Retrieved from http://www.nga.org/files/live/sites/NGA/files/pdf/0702INNOVATIONSTEM.PDF

National Research Council. (1996). *National science education standards.* Washington, DC: National Academies Press.

About the Author

Beth L. Andrews has worked with gifted learners in grades 1–7 for almost 30 years. During that time, she has served educators as a mentor teacher, a gifted and talented educational consultant, a coordinator of gifted programs, and an author of curriculum for gifted learners. Beth is a former president of the Orange County Council for Gifted Education and is currently the Technology Chair and Educator Representative for the California Association for the Gifted. Beth has provided professional development in the area of giftedness for more than 20 years, having presented on numerous topics related to gifted education and worked with hundreds of teachers.